E. M. (Eliza Maria) Jones

**Dairying for Profit**

Or, The Poor Man's Cow

E. M. (Eliza Maria) Jones

**Dairying for Profit**
*Or, The Poor Man's Cow*

ISBN/EAN: 9783744791571

Printed in Europe, USA, Canada, Australia, Japan

Cover: Foto ©Andreas Hilbeck / pixelio.de

More available books at **www.hansebooks.com**

# DAIRYING FOR PROFIT;

OR,

## THE POOR MAN'S COW.

BY

## MRS. E. M. JONES.

———— ·◆· ————

MONTREAL.

JOHN LOVELL & SON.

—

1892.

# INTRODUCTION.

In the winter of 1891-1892, I was requested by Mr. Hugh Graham, of Montreal, Publisher of the Family Herald and Weekly Star, to write some articles on Dairy Matters, for his paper.

To fully appreciate the compliment paid me, one would need to know the enormous and rapidly increasing circulation of this great paper.

As a result, I received so many kindly letters about my Dairy Articles and so many requests for further information, that it led to my collecting the letters with some others I had written, and adding to them all I thought necessary to cover the ground.

I earnestly hope the little book will be found readable, and still more do I hope that it will be useful.

I offer this work with a keen sense of its crudeness and its many faults, but I hope the public will extend to it the same kindly welcome they have always accorded to all my efforts.

ELIZA M. JONES.

Brockville, Ont., Can.,
May 9, 1892.

# INDEX.

## CHAPTER XI.

## CHAPTER XII.

## CHAPTER XIII.

## CHAPTER XIV.

## CHAPTER XV.

## CHAPTER XVI.

# CHAPTER I.

## ON CHOOSING A COW.

In no branch of farming is there such deplorable waste and short-sightedness as in dairying—such a large amount of labor for so small a result, and that result, too, of a very indifferent quality.

Farmers of to-day are barely existing who ought to be in comfortable circumstances; while those are barely comfortable who ought to be rich, and this with only the same facilities as they now enjoy.

The cause of this trouble is, mainly, misapplied labor, going the wrong way to work, toiling over things that don't pay.

The object in writing this book is to offer to hard-working, practical farmers some suggestions by which they may increase their incomes, multiply their comforts, and better their position; to present to them facts and figures that will bear the closest scrutiny, and to give them a brief sketch of a life spent in dairying; a life marked by many mistakes and occasional failures, but also crowned with success beyond my expectations, and cheered by such kindly appreciation and such complimentary notices as are far beyond my deserts.

Some may ask why I wish to record my failures.

In reply, I would quote to them an old Scotch story:—

An auld wife remarked that she " didna think the Scriptures were aye a safe guide, for David was held up as an exawmple to us a', when he was a sinfu' mon."

" Hoots, woman," said her neighbor, " David wasna pit there as an exawmple at a'; he was just meant for a light-house, to warn us aff the rocks."

And so, if the record of my failures and mistakes will only serve the same purpose, I shall not have written in vain, and I may be of as much practical use as those who quote only their successes and bury their failures out of sight, making no sign to others to " warn them aff the rocks."

Now, I don't mean to divide my lecture into as many "heads and particulars " as one old Scotch minister used to do in Glasgow, for I invariably went to sleep under them, and I am afraid my readers might do the same.

But some divisions of the subject are necessary, and they are chiefly three :—

1. The choice of a good cow ;
2. The keeping and feeding of her, to the best advantage ;
3. The most profitable way of caring for and marketing her product.

On the choice of your dairy cow, whether you breed her or buy her, depends the whole success of your dairy. You wouldn't wish to use the old-fashioned wooden plough of our forefathers, nor to go back to the flail, for " it's ill working with poor tools."

And the poorest tool on the face of the earth is a poor cow.

It is not only that she is no profit, it is worse than that—she runs you in debt.

Still worse is the case if the poor cow be one of a herd, and for this reason : If a person keeps but one cow he very soon knows if she be good or bad, but if he keeps a good many, the worthless cow is not so readily detected. She may be a smooth-looking animal, and may even give a fair flow of milk, and yet she may not only fall short of paying for her keep, but be eating up all the profit made by her neighbor, and so the farmer has not a cent of gain on the pair.

And the useless cow is not only deteriorating as years go by, but is perpetuating her worthless kind, to the loss of her owner and to the detriment of all the country around.

The form and features of a good dairy cow have been so often described that only a brief mention is needed here, but some points are so essential that they can hardly be too strongly impressed.

A good cow must be long, level, and loose-jointed, with a capacious body, short, fine legs, long, light neck, clean cut and intelligent head, thin withers, deep flank, thin, flat thighs, and rich, soft, mellow skin, showing a deep orange color under any white markings, and inside of ear.

As viewed from the side, she must present a perfect wedge shape, exceedingly deep behind and very light in front, and, as viewed from behind, she must show ample room to carry a large, full udder with ease and without chafing. No cow can do this that is of a beefy conformation and that has not a good "arch."

The udder itself must be soft and silky, free from warts and from

# PREFACE.

To the farmers' wives of America, this little book is dedicated—to my sisters in toil, the tired and over-tasked women, who are wearing their lives away in work which has little hope and less profit, and to whom the cares of the dairy form the "last straw" which breaks their already aching backs.

For many years I have been receiving letters from these weary sisters, in every State in the Union, in every Province of Canada, and their burden is always the same.

"We are *so tired*, cannot you help us? You are a woman like us, but your cattle have won a great reputation, your dairy has been a success, and your butter sells at a fine price.' How did you do it?"

Replying to all these letters has grown into a task beyond any one person's time and strength; and to give all the information asked for, I would have to write a little book to each one.

Therefore, I have resolved that I *will* write the little book, and have it printed, and sold at so low a price as to be within the reach of every one who keeps one cow or a hundred.

If I could go into every farmer's house in America, and say, " I can show you :

" 1st. How to make ⅓ more and far better butter than you do now;

" 2nd. At a less cost for keeping cattle ;

" 3rd. With less labor on cattle and dairy utensils ;

" 4th. And how to sell your butter for ⅓ more money than you are getting for it now," I would, indeed, be a welcome guest.

All this I *can* do, not in person, but by this little book, and so I send it out to my fellow-women, with earnest wishes for their approval.

If I can lighten the labors of even a few tired women and cheer their lives and put some money in their pockets, then I shall not have written in vain.

ELIZA M. JONES.

Brockville, Ont., Can., April 15, 1892.

long, coarse hair.   It must extend *well* forward and reach well up behind, having nothing of a globular shape.   It must be square, level beneath, and not too deeply quartered, with teats of good size, evenly placed, very far apart both ways, and of uniform size.   The udder must be very large and handsome when full, and when empty must be loose and soft, the rear part lying in folds—in fact, as the saying goes, it should almost "milk out to nothing."   Such an udder is capable of great distension without discomfort to the animal, and adds wonderfully, not only to the appearance, but to the intrinsic value of the dairy cow.

The milk veins should be exceedingly large and crooked, and the milk yielded easily and evenly all round.

Avoid a cow very hard and tough to milk.   She is a continual nuisance.   Still worse is the one that leaks her milk.

Avoid a very thick-skinned cow, whose hide is inclined to stick to her ribs, or, on the other hand, one whose hide is too thin and paper-like, indicating delicacy of constitution.

In an animal that "handles well" there is a peculiar soft, loose, velvety touch, that is quickly learnt by experience, and without which no animal can be really thrifty.

If, with all these good qualities, you get a cow that is young, healthy, with a soft, silky coat of hair, and one with a gentle, placid temper, you may be assured that you have made the first step on the road to success, even if she has cost you a little more than your neighbor has paid for an indifferent cow.

Taking the common cattle of the country as a basis, if you pay $30 for a cow that runs you $10 in debt by the end of the year, and that gives you a calf no better than she is herself, it is a poor speculation.

But if, on the other hand, you pay $50 for a cow that shows you $30 profit at the year's end, as such a cow should do, that is a pleasure to look at and a satisfaction to own, and that gives you a calf still better than herself, you have made the best and safest investment in a farmer's power.

In putting money at interest, you would think yourself very lucky to get $5 a year on $50.   From one cow you should get $30 a year on $50, and not only have the cow herself in good order, but a valuable calf besides.   And as you spend no more time in milking and feeding the good cow than the poor one, it is easy to see on which side your bread is buttered.

# CHAPTER II.

### ON FEEDING AND CARING FOR THE COW.

Having bought your cow, the next thing is, what to do with her.

On no account make any sudden change from her previous food, but let such things be done gradually. If it be summer, turn the new cow into a fair pasture where there is water; treat gently and milk regularly, and she will soon be contented and happy in her new home. If it be winter, put her in a warm, comfortable stable, with plenty of clean dry straw for bedding, water her and feed her a warm bran mash and plenty of good hay.

Then make up your mind what to feed your cow, and gradually work up to that quantity.

For a fresh calved cow, giving 16 to 20 quarts of milk a day, I have found nothing better than the following treatment :—

At half-past 5 a.m. the stall is cleaned out, and cow cleaned off, rubbing the udder with a large, coarse but soft cloth. If necessary to wash the udder, do it with tepid water, and be careful to dry it thoroughly or it will soon get rough and sore. Give the cow a large armful of hay, and then milk her as quickly and as quietly as you can, taking every drop you can possibly get from her. Of the manner of milking and the care of the milk we will speak hereafter.

The next thing is to feed your cow.

I will here give the ration we use as a basis, but it is varied according to circumstances and prices of feed. I also give prices in our locality, and these will be found to average much the same everywhere, and to maintain the same value, in proportion to the prices of dairy products :—

|  | cts. |
|---|---|
| 10 lbs. ground oats at $20 per ton...... | 10 |
| 8 lbs. bran at $12.50 per ton.... | 5 |
| 4 lbs. cornmeal at $25 per ton.... | 5 |
| 4 lbs. pea meal at $25 per ton..... | 5 |
| 16 lbs. hay at $10 per ton...... | 8 |
| Cost of feed per day...... | 33 |

Some of the hay is run through a cutter, and mixed with the grain which has all been thoroughly mixed together. This is then divided into three feeds, and given at morning, noon and night. The mixture is put in a large stable bucket, with a very little salt, and enough boiling water is poured on to wet it all through. It is then covered with an old bag, or rug, and left to steep for an hour. Then add enough water (either cold or tepid, as required) to make a nice, large, warm, comfortable mash, rather thin, and see how greedily the cow will eat it, and how contented she will look afterwards.

Now, the cow should be thoroughly cleaned with a card and a good brush, and not one speck of dirt or any stain left on her.

Some people boast that they keep the cow's udder clean, and perhaps they do, but all the rest of the animal is left in a filthy condition.

This dirt dries into the hair, and then the act of milking shakes it down, like dust, into the pail, rendering the milk unfit for human food.

You may now, with a clear conscience, leave your cow to rest and digest her food, and if you have shaken up her bed and removed everything that is wet or soiled, you cannot help feeling pretty well satisfied, as you take a parting look at her; especially is this the case if it be mid-winter.

You think of other unfortunate cattle, out in the barn-yard, or even in the field, knee deep in snow or mud, with a bitter wind whistling around their gaunt frames.

You see them devouring part of the manure pile, or trying to drink from a frozen puddle, and a filthy one at that.

You see the rough, shaggy coat, the arched back, the withered up udder and the general look of wretchedness, and you cannot help wishing that death would end the sufferings of the poor brute.

Then, with such a satisfied pleasure, you think of your own cow.

After a comfortable night's rest in a warm and dry but airy stable, she has had her good hot breakfast and her feed of hay. Her large, beautiful udder has made it a pleasure to milk her, and the fine pail of rich milk has testified to a good cow and a generous owner.

As day advances, and the sun shines into your barn through large windows, you see your cow lying down, chewing her cud, her bedding abundant, dry and clean, her coat spotless, smooth and soft, her nose moist, her large, gentle eyes full and bright, and her whole looks full of placid content.

And you have the comfort of feeling that it is not a costly pleasure to see her so, for that your cow not only pays you back every cent you lay out on her, but is putting a good profit into your pocket in hard cash every week of her life. I have often thought that over every cow's stall should be written three lines:

"A good man is merciful to his beast."
"Cleanliness is next to Godliness."
"IT PAYS, IT PAYS, IT PAYS."

And write the last line in capital letters, for on it hang all the law and the doctrines in the farmer's mind.

At noon your cow gets as much water as she likes to drink, and in *very* cold weather, if the chill be taken off it, and a handful of bran stirred in, it will be so much more money in your pocket. Then she gets her mash and a small feed of hay. In the evening she gets watered and fed, and is milked; any dirt on her skin is removed, the stall cleaned out, fresh bedding added, and, with a good feed of sweet hay before her, she is left for the night, and her owner may go to bed and sleep the sleep of the just.

# CHAPTER III.

## ONE YEAR'S YIELD OF A GRADE JERSEY.

In my last chapter I gave a generous feed ration for a cow in flush of milk, said ration costing 33 cents per day.

" Thirty-three cents a day to feed a cow," I hear some hard-fisted farmer exclaim ; " that ends the business. Only rich people can go in for tom-foolery like that, we poor farmers can't afford it."

Neighbor farmers and friends, you *can* afford it, as I will prove to you.

The money is not spent, sunk out of sight; it is only invested, put out at interest, and it speedily comes back to you, *doubled.*

This book is not written for rich people, who can afford to overfeed, or to underfeed, a cow, and never ask or care whether their fancy farm pays.

It is written for people who, like you and me, have *got to* make it pay, or else give it up.

*It is the poor man who can't afford to keep a poor cow.*

And it is the poor man, above all others, who can't afford to be slip-shod in this matter, but who has *got to* know exactly just what every cow on his place consumes, and what it costs.

Also, just what every cow produces and what it sells for. Then the profit or loss is at once apparent.

The profits can be steadily increased to their utmost limit, and the losses promptly and effectually stopped, showing a satisfactory balance sheet at the end of the year.

But in order to do this an account must be kept. You don't want a gilt-edged note-book, nor an intricate system of bookkeeping, nor much extra labor, after a long hard day's work.

But you *do* want to know what you are doing, and how you stand.

What on earth is the good of slaving and toiling, from daylight to dark, if you don't make anything by it ?

And how can you stop a leak if you don't know where it is ?

Of course every farmer will tell you that he has a "sort of" idea, he "kinder keeps the run of it;" but that won't do. It reminds me of a story I read not long ago:

A newly married couple started housekeeping, and the husband urged the wife to keep an account. She gladly consented, and he gave her a little book, telling her to put down on one side what cash she received, and on the opposite page to enter what she spent.

Long afterwards he asked her how the book balanced, and she promptly replied that "it balanced exactly."

Somewhat surprised, as the little wife was neither experienced nor accurate in money matters, he asked to see the book.

On one side, under the correct date, appeared this entry: "Rec'd. from Larry—$500."

On the opposite side was simply one entry, in good big letters, "Spent it all!"

Now, we can't afford to balance our books in that way.

On one side we must enter every cent received from our cows, in any way, and must also put down, as closely as we can estimate it, all milk, cream and butter consumed in the family, and put it at market prices.

On the other side appears every bit of feed consumed, whether purchased or raised on the place.

And, just here, let me caution you against one error. You will often hear a farmer say, when accused of keeping a poor cow that doesn't pay for her keep, "Oh well, she don't cost me much to keep; we grow all the stuff ourselves."

My friends, that is one of the biggest mistakes we make.

It is not the question, "What *did it cost* us to grow this load of hay?" but "*What cash price can I get for this hay in the market?*" And whatever is its market value (less the cost of drawing it there), that is the value of the hay you are feeding to your cow, that is what it costs to keep her.

Now, figure on that basis, and see if she pays. Sometimes she does, and sometimes she does not, but it is mostly not.

What are the reasons?

Poor cows, poor keep, poor butter.

I have endeavored to meet the first difficulty, by showing the importance of choosing a really good cow.

And in this book I shall try to prove to you the economy and wisdom of feeding her well, and shall try to prove that it pays.

I cannot do better than to give the actual figures, taken from my own books. A splendid cow was put in my stable, just fresh in milk, the 1st of October. She was in grand condition, and had always been well fed and cared for. Consequently she was able to go on to a splendid piece of after-grass, and to take a goodly ration of grain as well.

Now, in making out my estimate, I am leaving out fractions as being easier for me to write and for others to follow me, and yet sufficiently accurate for all practical purposes.

During October I fed my cow besides grass :

| | |
|---|---|
| 5 lbs. ground oats per day..................... | 5 cts. |
| 4 lbs. " corn " ..................... | 5 cts. |
| 4 lbs. " peas " ..................... | 5 cts. |
| Total........................... | 15 cts. per day. |

She needed no hay, as the grass was so good. During November, December and January I fed her daily :

| | |
|---|---|
| 7 lbs. ground oats............................ | 7 cts. |
| 8 lbs. bran.................................. | 5 cts. |
| 4 lbs. ground corn........................... | 5 cts. |
| 4 lbs. ground peas........................... | 5 cts. |
| 16 lbs. hay................................. | 8 cts. |
| Total........................... | 30 cts. a day. |

During February, March and April, I fed her :

| | |
|---|---|
| 4 lbs. ground oats............................ | 4 cts. |
| 2 lbs. " corn............................ | 2½ cts. |
| 2 lbs. " peas............................ | 2½ cts. |
| 4 lbs. bran.................................. | 2½ cts. |
| 16 lbs. hay................................. | 8 cts. |
| Total........................... | 19½ cts. per day. |

During May and June she was on grass, requiring no hay, but she had daily :

| | |
|---|---|
| 2 lbs. ground corn........................... | 2½ cts. |
| 2 lbs. " peas........................... | 2½ cts. |
| Total........................... | 5 cts. per day. |

As she was now only three months from calving, all grain was taken from her, but as grass was good, and the cow in splendid order, she gave a good yield of milk and butter (as will be seen in next table) through July and half of August, when she was just dry, and had six weeks' rest, and then calved again.

It need hardly be said that the butter from this cow was exceptionally fine. During seven months, from 1st October to end of April, I sold it for 30 cents a pound, and the rest of the time for 25 cents. (This was before I kept registered Jerseys.)

Now, we can soon see how my cow and I stood at the end of the year, by referring to the annexed table, giving her monthly yield and cost of her keep:

| Cost of keep in addition to Pasture. | Yield of Butter, lbs. | Price. |
|---|---|---|
| October..................... $4.50 | 60 at 30 cts. | $18.00 |
| November ................ 9.00 | 50    " | 15.00 |
| December................. 9.00 | 40    " | 12.00 |
| January .................. 9.00 | 40    " | 12.00 |
| February ................ 6.00 | 32    " | 9.60 |
| March.................... 6.00 | 32    " | 9.60 |
| April...................... 6.00 | 30    " | 9.00 |
| May....................... 1.50 | 30 at 25 cts. | 7.50 |
| June....................... 1.50 | 30    " | 7.50 |
| July....................... .... | 20    " | 5.00 |
| August .................. .... | 8    " | 2.00 |
| September................ .... | .. | .... |
|  | | |
| $52.50 | 372 lbs. | $107.20 |
| Pasture................ 5.00 | | 57.50 |
|  | | |
| $57.50 | Profit...... | $49.70 |

I considered this a good showing, but I assure you it was not my first attempt at dairying, I had worked up to it by degrees, acquiring experience as I went. And I could have made no such record with a poor cow, but I will speak of this point in my next chapter.

# CHAPTER IV.

## WHAT IS THE BEST BUTTER BREED?

I think I hear many of my readers ask this question, and I will answer it as honestly as I can. I experimented for years with many different breeds, having no prejudice in any way, either for or against any of them, except in one case.

Hailing, as I do, " frae the land o' caikes," or, as I like better to put it, from " the Land o' the Leal," I must confess to a life-long fondness for a good Ayrshire cow.

Their beauty and docility, their great yield of milk, and their hardy constitutions place them almost the first on the list of dairy cattle, in my opinion.

With all my heart, I wish I could write them first, but it would be false to my convictions.

They are a truly magnificent breed, but there is one cow in the world that I think is still better in the dairy, and that is the little Channel Island cow, be she Jersey, Guernsey, or Alderney. They are all, virtually, the same breed, raised under the same rules and restrictions, and by reason not only of their marvellous yield of butter, but from the wonderful quality of that butter, the Jersey cow stands to-day in the proud position of queen of the dairy.

If I didn't keep Jerseys I would keep Ayrshires, but I have got to confess that the Jerseys are ahead, for one situated as I am.

I don't mean to detract one bit from the merits of my favorites, the Ayrshires,—no, indeed, " It's not that I love Jemima less, but I love doughnuts more," and now I will give my reasons for it: I faithfully tried Ayrshires, Shorthorns (of good milking strains), native cows, and different grades, and, while attaining good results, I found there was still much to be desired, a good deal in quantity, but more, very much more, in quality.

And so, after many years' labor and testing, I at last got a grade Jersey, which is the cow referred to in my last chapter, and every one,

I think, will admit that the butter yield is grand, especially in view of the food consumed. But she had a large share of Ayrshire blood in her, besides being half Jersey.

I plainly state, that for every one who makes butter, I think the Channel Island cattle the most paying, not only on account of quantity, but *much* more on account of *quality*, which is, certainly, superlative.

But everyone must be their own judge in this matter.

Now, as to my preference for Jerseys, I will give a few reasons, so that the public may know *why* I like them.

Some people object, that the Jersey gives so little milk as compared with other cows.

This is entirely different from my experience. Not only does a good Jersey give a fine mess of milk, when fresh, but she holds to it throughout the year in a way totally unknown to other breeds, and some Jerseys never go dry for years.

It is this *persistent milking* of such rich milk, and this large and continuous yield of butter of most exquisite quality, that renders the Jersey, *par excellence*, the family cow. Perhaps I can better convince my readers by giving a few figures.

The grade cow referred to in the previous chapter was not only tested for butter, but *every milking* was weighed, all through the year, and she gave exactly 7,756 lbs. of milk in eleven months. This sold at the usual average price would bring in $200 a year, less the cost of keeping the cow.

Being so pleased with grades, I resolved to purchase some pure Jerseys, which I did, seventeen years ago, and every succeeding year since then has only confirmed and strengthened my opinion, that the Jersey, for both milk and butter, is the most profitable cow in all the world.

A two-year old heifer, well cared for with me, will make more butter than those of same age of any breed I ever knew. For instance, here are some tests in my herd :

Orange Delia, 2 years, $9\frac{1}{2}$ lbs. per week ; Miss Daisy Delle, 2 years, $10\frac{1}{2}$ lbs. per week ; Charlotte Hertedy, 2 years, $8\frac{1}{2}$ lbs. per week ; Topsey of Malone, 2 years, $14\frac{1}{2}$ lbs. per week ; Bessie of Malone, 21 months, $10\frac{1}{2}$ lbs. per week ; Jetsam's May, first prize 3-year old at Toronto, Ottawa and Montreal, also sweepstakes, as best of any age, at Montreal, and in my first prize herd at the Montreal Exhibition last September, made me, the year before, at only 2 years old, 14 lbs. 5 oz. a week, thus pretty well endorsing the judge's opinion ; Belle Temple 2nd, 2 years, 14 lbs. a week ; Charming of St. Lambert, 2 years, 15¼ lbs. a week; Lilium Excelsium 2nd, 2 years, 10½ lbs. a week.

These are only a very few of the two-year-old tests I have made, and most of these heifers, after milking for nine months, were still making 1 lb. per day of splendid butter. In older cows a few of the tests are :

Eugenic 2nd, 14 lbs. a week ; Imported Mulberry, 14¼ lbs. a week ; Brown Mulberry, 14 lbs. a week; Silver Delle, 17¼ lbs. a week; Belle Stenben, 17 lbs. a week; Lilium Excelsium, 17½ lbs. a week; Princess Clothilde, 17¼ lbs. a week ; Sibyl's Lass, 14 lbs. a week; Rioter's Queen, 17½ lbs. a week; Lisgar's Ella, 17½ lbs. a week ; Diana of St. Lambert, 16 lbs. a week ; Bertha Black (at rate of), 23 lbs. 10 oz. a week ; Maggie Rex (at rate of), 21 lbs. 7 oz. a week; Miss Satanella, 20 lbs. 6 oz. a week on second calf only.

Now, these are all sworn tests, made either under my direct super-vision, or made entirely by myself, in person, and they are only a very few of those I could report. Is it any wonder, then, that I should prefer the Jersey cow ?

I don't say that no other breed will make the same quantity of butter on same quantity of feed.

But I do say, that I never could get them to do it, or nearly to do it, and I think I understand the matter pretty well.

In conclusion, it has been urged that Jerseys are delicate and soon wear out. I can offer no better refutation than to submit the test of my grand old cow, Massena, after she had entered her sixteenth year, and then leave farmers to draw their own conclusions.

In her sixteenth year Massena has yielded, in six months only, 5413½ pounds milk, from which has been actually churned 416 lbs. 10 oz. splendid butter.

| 1891. | MILK. | BUTTER. |
|---|---|---|
| | lbs. | lbs. oz. |
| March 6..28 | | 3 8 |
| March 7..30 | | |
| March 8..30½ | | 3 9 |
| March 9..31 | | |
| March 10..31½ | | 3 11 |
| March 11..30½ | | |
| March 12..30 | | 4 4 |
| March 13..32½ | | |
| March 14..32 | | 4 9 |
| March 15..33 | | |
| March 16..33 | | 4 11 |
| March 17..33½ | | |
| March 18..34 | | 5 2 |
| March 19..33½ | | |
| March 20..33½ | | 5 2½ |
| March 21..32½ | | |
| March 22..33 | | 5 4 |
| March 23..32½ | | |
| March 24..31½ | | 5 2½ |
| March 25..33½ | | |
| March 26..34 | | 5 0 |
| March 27..33 | | |
| March 28..33 | | 5 2½ |
| March 29..33 | | |
| March 30..32½ | | 5 1½ |
| March 31..26½ | | |
| April 1..33 | | 5 1 |
| April 2..31 | | |
| April 3..30½ | | 5 1½ |
| April 4..32 | | |
| April 5..32½ | | 5 0 |
| April 6..32½ | | |
| April 7..31 | | 5 2 |
| April 8..31 | | |
| April 9..31 | | 4 11 |
| April 10..29½ | | |
| April 11..29 | | 4 15 |
| April 12..27½ | | |
| April 13..28 | | 4 14 |
| April 14..29 | | |
| April 15..29½ | | 4 15 |
| April 16..30 | | |
| April 17..29 | | 4 15 |
| April 18..29 | | |
| April 19..29½ | | 4 15 |
| April 20..29½ | | |
| April 21..30 | | 4 12 |
| April 22..29 | | |
| April 23..28 | | 4 8 |
| April 24..23½ | | |

| 1891. | MILK. | BUTTER. |
|---|---|---|
| | lbs. | lbs. oz. |
| April 25..22 | | 4 2½ |
| April 26..20 | | |
| April 27..22 | | 4 3 |
| April 28..26 | | |
| April 29..26½ | | 4 1½ |
| April 30..26½ | | |
| May 1..26 | | 4 8 |
| May 2..26½ | | |
| May 3..26½ | | 4 7 |
| May 4..25½ | | |
| May 5..28½ | | 4 8½ |
| May 6..29½ | | |
| May 7..29½ | | 4 9½ |
| May 8..30½ | | |
| May 9..31 | | 4 8½ |
| May 10..30½ | | |
| May 11..30½ | | 4 7 |
| May 12..30½ | | |
| May 13..30½ | | 4 7 |
| May 14..30½ | | |
| May 15..30½ | | 4 6½ |
| May 16..30 | | |
| May 17..30½ | | 4 8 |
| May 18..30½ | | |
| May 19..30½ | | 4 7½ |
| May 20..30½ | | |
| May 21..29½ | | 4 8½ |
| May 22..29½ | | |
| May 23..30½ | | 4 11 |
| May 24..30 | | |
| May 25..30 | | 4 9½ |
| May 26..30 | | |
| May 27..30 | | 4 9 |
| May 28..31 | | |
| May 29..30½ | | 4 10 |
| May 30..30½ | | |
| May 31..30½ | | 4 8½ |
| June 1..30 | | |
| June 2..29 | | 4 9½ |
| June 3..30 | | |
| June 4..30 | | 4 7½ |
| June 5..30 | | |
| June 6..30 | | 4 8½ |
| June 7..30½ | | |
| June 8..29½ | | 4 7½ |
| June 9..30 | | |
| June 10..30 | | 4 8½ |
| June 11..30 | | |
| June 12..29½ | | 4 8 |
| June 13..30 | | |

| 1891. | MILK. | BUTTER. | | 1891. | MILK. | BUTTER. | |
|---|---|---|---|---|---|---|---|
| | lbs. | lbs. | oz. | | lbs. | lbs. | oz. |
| June 14..30 | | | | July 26..28 | | | |
| June 15..29½ | | 4 | 7½ | July 27..27 | | 4 | 5½ |
| June 16..30 | | | | July 28..28 | | | |
| June 17..30 | | 4 | 9½ | July 29..28 | | 4 | 6½ |
| June 18..30 | | | | July 30..28 | | | |
| June 19..30 | | 4 | 8½ | July 31..28½ | | 4 | 7 |
| June 20..30 | | | | Aug. 1..30 | | | |
| June 21..28½ | | 4 | 6½ | Aug. 2..29 | | 4 | 7 |
| June 22..30 | | | | Aug. 3..30 | | | |
| June 23..29½ | | 4 | 7½ | Aug. 4..28½ | | 4 | 6½ |
| June 24..29 | | | | Aug. 5..29 | | | |
| June 25..29 | | 4 | 6½ | Aug. 6..28½ | | 4 | 7 |
| June 26..28½ | | | | Aug. 7..29 | | | |
| June 27..29 | | 4 | 7 | Aug. 8..29 | | 4 | 6 |
| June 28..29½ | | | | Aug. 9..28½ | | | |
| June 29..28½ | | 4 | 7 | Aug. 10..28½ | | 4 | 5½ |
| June 30..29½ | | | | Aug. 11..28½ | | | |
| July 1..28½ | | 4 | 6 | Aug. 12..27½ | | 4 | 7½ |
| July 2..29½ | | | | Aug. 13..28½ | | | |
| July 3..28½ | | 4 | 6½ | Aug. 14..27 | | 4 | 6½ |
| July 4..29 | | | | Aug. 15..27½ | | | |
| July 5..28½ | | 4 | 7½ | Aug. 16..28 | | 4 | 6½ |
| July 6..29 | | | | Aug. 17..28 | | | |
| July 7..29½ | | 4 | 8 | Aug. 18..28½ | | 4 | 7 |
| July 8..30 | | | | Aug. 19..28 | | | |
| July 9..30½ | | 4 | 8 | Aug. 20..29 | | 4 | 6 |
| July 10..29½ | | | | Aug. 21..27½ | | | |
| July 11..29 | | 4 | 7½ | Aug. 22..28½ | | 4 | 5½ |
| July 12..30 | | | | Aug. 23..27½ | | | |
| July 13..29½ | | 4 | 7 | Aug. 24..28 | | 4 | 6 |
| July 14..29½ | | | | Aug. 25..28 | | | |
| July 15..29½ | | 4 | 8½ | Aug. 26..28 | | 4 | 6½ |
| July 16..29 | | | | Aug. 27..28 | | | |
| July 17..32 | | 4 | 6½ | Aug. 28..27½ | | 4 | 5½ |
| July 18..28½ | | | | Aug. 29..28 | | | |
| July 19..29 | | 4 | 7½ | Aug. 30..28 | | 4 | 5 |
| July 20..29 | | | | Aug. 31..27½ | | | |
| July 21..29 | | 4 | 8 | Sept. 1..27½ | | 4 | 7 |
| July 22..30 | | | | Sept. 2..29 | | | |
| July 23..29 | | 4 | 7 | Sept. 3..28 | | 4 | 4½ |
| July 24..28 | | | | Sept. 4..27½ | | | |
| July 25..27½ | | 4 | 6½ | Sept. 5..27½ | | 4 | 4 |
| | | | | Total lbs. Milk. | 5413½ | 416 | 10 |

For 6 consecutive months Massena thus averaged over 29 lbs. of milk a day, and for 6 consecutive months she has averaged 16 lbs. of butter every week. If any cow but a Jersey will do this, I have never seen it. But this is why I keep Jerseys.

The next month her yield was *estimated* only, as she was away at the Fairs.

We took the average yield of August, the month before she went away, and of October, the month after she returned, to arrive at her yield when away.

On this basis her whole year's record was as follows:

|  | MILK. lbs. | BUTTER lbs. | oz. |
|---|---|---|---|
| March 7th to Sept. 6th, inclusive, just 6 mos., the cow actually yielded...... ...... ...... ...... | 5,413½ | 416 | 10 |
| Sept. 7th to Oct. 6th, estimated ...... ...... ...... | 751½ | 61 | 4¾ |
| Oct. 7th to Nov. 6th, actual...... ...... ...... | 629 | 54 | 8 |
| Nov. 7th to Dec. 6th, actual...... ...... ...... ...... | 590½ | 51 | 15 |
| Dec. 7th to Jan. 6th, actual...... ...... ...... | 505½ | 43 | 1½ |
| Jan. 7th to Feb. 6th, actual...... ...... ...... | 333 | 21 | 4½ |
| Feb. 7th to 15th, 9 days, actual...... ...... ...... | 67½ | 5 | 5 |
| Total for 11 mos. and 9 days...... ...... ...... | 8,290½ | 654 | ¾ |

From February 15th her milk was thrown out, till the morning of the 28th, when she dropped a fine heifer calf sired by her own son, Massena's Son, that had such a glorious success at our exhibitions last fall.

To return to Massena's test. It was made during her sixteenth year; she had dropped two mature calves inside of a year.

She had traveled over 1,100 miles by rail, within the year, and stood three weeks on Fair grounds. She had been in no way forced, as being far too valuable; for nearly two months before calving she had no grain whatever. During the nineteen weeks previous to calving she averaged over 9¼ lbs. butter a week, and for the whole period, until the last seven weeks (when she was only eating thin bran) it took but 11½ lbs. of her milk to make 1 lb. of butter. What cow of her age can beat the record?

# CHAPTER V.

CHOOSE THE BREED WHICH YOU ARE SURE SUITS YOUR WANTS BEST.
—IMPROVING OUR DAIRY STANDING.—EXPERIMENTAL
FARM AT OTTAWA, ONT., CAN.

Do not, however, think that I am blind to the merits of any cow but a Jersey.

Far from it.

## "A GOOD COW *IS* A GOOD COW, ALL THE WORLD OVER, BE SHE WHAT BREED SHE MAY."

It is not the object of this book to advertise my Jerseys, I have no need and no wish to do so in this way; it is better done in the proper channel.

My sole aim in writing this is to induce people to select and to keep only the *very best* cattle of their kinds ; to show them (as far as I know myself) how to make *more* butter and far *better* butter than ever before, and also how to market it to better advantage, so as to net them more money; to awaken Canadian farmers to the fact that they are not keeping up with the procession, and to show them that every year thousands of dollars which ought to go into their own pockets are paid out by England to Irish and Danish dairymen.

We don't make half enough butter, in view of the number of cows in the Dominion, and what we *do* make is not nearly as good as it ought to be.

And there is no excuse for this state of affairs. There is more thoroughbred stock in the country than ever before, and at lower prices.

The economy and advantages of the silo are now so well understood, that farms can carry at least one-third more stock, and at less expense.

And, best of all, we have in the Experimental Farm at Ottawa, and its various branches, one of the grandest institutions of the age, one originated expressly for farmers and dairymen, and maintained for their benefit at an annual expense of about $80,000.00.

If, with all these advantages, Canadians cannot put the dairy product of their country on the footing that really belongs to it, they have no one but themselves to blame.

To return to the sort of cattle kept.

It is folly to exalt one breed at the expense of another, and to deny the good qualities which they undoubtedly possess.

People so narrow-minded will never make much progress, either in dairying or in anything else, and even their favorite breed will soon deteriorate in their hands, because they are not open to conviction, they refuse to compare notes with their neighbors, and they won't keep up with the times.

They are like the egotist who said that there were only two kinds of dog in the world, the dogs that he owned himself and the curs that every one else owned!

Do not be so prejudiced, but recognize merit wherever you see it, and give it its due.

It is my *honest conviction* that the Jersey is the best paying cow in the world, and that she will make far more and better butter than any other on the same amount of feed, or less.

If I did not think this, why should I keep them?

However, I want no one to pin their faith to mine.

Look about you, make tests and experiments, and then bring common sense to bear on the matter.

Only, let me warn you about one thing, carry your experiments far enough to be perfectly *sure* of your ground, otherwise you may be greatly misled.

" One swallow doesn't make a summer," neither does one experiment prove a thing. In fact, the second experiment often contradicts the first.

Why is this, you ask?

Because experiments are so largely affected by circumstances, some of which we know nothing about, and others that we know all about but cannot control.

A *great many* experiments, however, will soon determine a point beyond a shadow of doubt.

This system it is, which gives such immense value to the experiments conducted by Professor Robertson and his colleagues at the Experimental Farm at Ottawa.

No fact is there announced as such, till it has been proved and proved again ; till it is absolutely impossible to question it, and till the public may safely accept it and feel quite sure that in following the Professor's directions they are on the right track.

As a result, it is hardly possible to estimate the benefit this Institution is proving to the agricultural population of the Dominion. The good effects are spreading so widely and rooting so deeply, that the whole nation lies under a debt of gratitude to the Hon. Mr. Carling and to those associated with them, and their names will live in the history of Canada long after they themselves shall have ceased to labor.

I will now give you this advice :

Having carefully determined which is the best breed of cattle *for you*, and which will best suit your surroundings and best pay for their keep, then get the *very best* specimens of that breed that you can possibly procure.

Don't waste your money, but don't haggle about the price of a really first-class animal.

One dollar saved by purchasing an inferior animal is generally *one hundred* dollars lost before the year is out.

If you can start with a small but choice herd of thoroughbreds you are fortunate, and are on the high road to success.

If you can only buy two, buy a pair, the *very best* you can get, and your thoroughbreds will gradually increase, while the rest of your herd will be graded up by degrees till your pleasure and your profit will surprise you.

If you can only buy *one* animal, let it be a thoroughbred male, and then you will soon be able to afford a choice female of the same sort, and will have made a good beginning.

# CHAPTER VI.

MILKING AND SKIMMING.—SETTING MILK.—SHALLOW PANS.—
CREAMERS.—SEPARATORS.

Having got the very best cow possible, and fed her in the best manner, the next step is to make the finest quality of butter, and then to market it in the most advantageous manner.

I have often been asked how I made such good butter, and my answer is, I don't go too much by any given rule.

It is not possible to have full control over atmosphere and other surroundings, therefore we must bring judgment and common sense to bear upon the matter.

On a bench in the barn should be placed large tin cans, with covers, one of them having a large round tin shaped like a steamer fitted to the top, and then the cover placed on that. Of course the bottom of this is a wire strainer. Milking is done as quickly and quietly as possible, care being taken to do it thoroughly and in a most cleanly manner. Such a thing as wetting the hands or the teats of the cows is never permitted; it is a filthy habit, and is most unnecessary.

Each cow's milk is strained into the can immediately, and covered at once, and as quickly as one can is filled it is taken to the dairy, *and there strained again.* In some places shallow setting is still practised, in which case the pans should be set in a cool dairy, or in a cellar that is used for nothing but milk. Keep this place as pure and sweet as possible; in hot weather, keep the windows open at night and closed during the day, and have wire screens over them constantly.

Now, some people will tell you to skim at the end of 24 or 36 hours, or to skim regularly, night and morning.

*Do nothing of the kind* if you want to work to the best advantage, but skim *exactly when the milk is fit.*

I know it is a little hard to go to your dairy, prepared to skim the milk and get the pans washed up and out of the way, and find the milk not ready for skimming, but it can't be helped. Leave it alone, and go back at noon, when it will probably be ready.

The best time to skim shallow pans is when the milk is JUST BEGIN-
NING to lopper or thicken in the bottom of the pan—has just com-
menced to sour. A little experience will soon teach when this is the
case. Then, with a spoon, loosen it all round the edge (never, *never* do
this with your finger, as is the disgusting habit of some people), set the
pan on the edge of your deep cream can, tip it a little, and the whole
thick sheet of cream, guided a little with your spoon, will slip off, quick
and clean, taking hardly any milk with it. This is by far the best and
quickest way of skimming shallow pans, and time is money in a large
dairy.

Never skim two milkings at the same time. If one is ready to skim
the other is not, or else one is too ripe.

In deep setting, things are different. With plenty of ice, the cream
is supposed to be all up in 12 hours in any of the good creamers now in
use, and no doubt it generally is. As the milk, by this method, is
almost entirely protected from atmospheric influences, and is held at a
steady temperature, the process is much more uniform, and it is possible
to have regular hours for drawing off the cream, without any fear of mistake or loss. This is worth knowing.

I cannot imagine any one who has a bit of feeling for the females
of his household doing without a creamer, for the labor it saves is truly
surprising, and, to put it on no higher grounds, *it is generally cheaper
to take care of one's wife than it is to bury her.*

And, besides, it is money in the farmer's own pocket, for more butter
and very much better butter can be made from a creamer than from
shallow setting.

I confess to a love of the old way—the rows of shining pans in the
cool, quiet dairy, the rich hue of the golden cream, and most decidedly
to the thick cream that will hardly pour out on my porridge or my
strawberries, cream that 'can be got in no other way than by shallow
setting, and I have made just as much and just as good butter from
shallow setting, when temperature and everything else was exactly
right. But that "when" tells the whole story. It is simply impossible to control these surroundings, and they are not just right more than
one-fourth of the time, and, therefore, we wisely take to the creamer,
which does all this for us and gives us a uniform product. Still better
is the centrifugal machine, or separator, as it is called, which separates

the cream and milk as soon as milking is done, and more thoroughly, all the year round, than can be done in any other way.

This mode saves the washing of many tins, and saves all the ice used for deep setting. The only disadvantage seems to be in the hand labor of turning the machine, where no steam power is used, but even this cannot outweigh the many advantages of the separator.

When the cream is drawn off you are again at the mercy of the atmosphere, and now you must keep your wits about you, for here is where much trouble creeps in.

Stir your can thoroughly down to the bottom, twice a day, or every time fresh cream is added, and keep it as cool as you possibly can (but on no account freeze it) till you have sufficient for a churning.

Now, you must raise it in summer to 60 degrees, in winter to 62 to 65, according to the temperature of the room you churn in.

Some people do this by putting the can near the kitchen stove, and then the butter is ruined before it goes into the churn. The side next the stove will be ever so much too hot, oily and greasy, while the other side is too cool, and the cream will absorb every odor of cooking and kitchen, to re-appear in the butter and tell the tale of ignorance or carelessness.

There is but one way to temper cream properly, and that is in a hot water bath.

Have a larger can than the cream can, and have ready a long wooden paddle, a common thermometer and a clean towel. Fill the larger can about half full of hot water (but not boiling), then set in the cream can, and instantly begin stirring constantly with the paddle, so none of the cream next the tin will get over-heated. The water must raise as high as the cream does, so all will be equally heated.

Have a light wire attached to your thermometer, and lower it to the middle of the cream can occasionally. Hold it there a few moments, then take out and wipe quickly, so as to clear the glass.

The moment the cream is of right temperature, lift out the can, stir for a few moments longer, cover with a clean towel, and put where it will remain at exactly the same temperature till fit to churn.

Of this fitness or ripeness much has been said or written, while the truth is that only experience can decide. Twenty-four hours has been fixed as the right time, but it is often more and often less. Stir two or three times a day, and watch closely, and you will hardly fail in hitting the right degree of sourness or ripeness. But before you put it into the churn, try it again with the thermometer to insure its being just right, for nothing is a greater source of vexation and trouble than churning at a wrong temperature. If the cream is too hot, the butter is spoiled; if too cold, you may churn in vain for hours, and lose your temper and your time.

# CHAPTER VII.

### CHURNING.—SALTING.

Having got your cream into the best possible condition for churning, proceed to scald your churn with water that is actually boiling. Then cool it with fresh water, put in your cream, and churn with a steady, regular movement, and not too fast.

In spite of all our care, it will be found that this business is easier in summer than in winter weather, partly because grass butter comes easier, and partly because of the higher and more uniform temperature. Fifteen to thirty minutes in summer, and thirty to forty-five minutes in winter, will generally bring the butter in fine order.

An experienced ear can tell when the butter has come, by the peculiar *washing* sound in the churn, quite different from the dull, heavy thud of the thick cream when it is first put in. Our grandmothers could tell fast enough by the look of the dasher as it worked up and down, but the dash churn is now a thing of the past, and we are well rid of it, because it brought the butter in huge lumps—in fact, one of the old-time rules was to "gather the butter" in the churn before it was lifted out.

It was then put into a wooden bowl, washed and re-washed, spread out, and rolled up again, and beaten and mashed with a ladle till nine-tenths of the butter was spoiled before it ever went on the table.

This is all wrong. I don't mean to say that good butter was never made in the old times, for we all know better, but it was made only by a few, and made under difficulties. It was made by those who fed their cattle so well, those who were so intelligent in their ideas and so cleanly in their habits, and they succeeded in spite of many drawbacks.

They used the greatest judgment in creaming and ripening and the greatest care in working the butter. They never slid the ladle over it, leaving a shiny, greasy surface behind and breaking the grain, but they pressed it carefully, and worked it no more than was absolutely necessary.

But they were the exception and not the rule, and good butter was the exception also and not the rule ; while if the system of to-day be followed, as set forth in our leading papers, and taught in our dairy schools, good butter will be the rule, and poor butter the exception.

Having irreverently demolished the system of our grandmothers, what are we to do? I answer, churn till the butter is in a granular form, till it is only as big as grains of wheat, and then stop; it is done.

Now, you have two objects in view : First, to keep it in that form, to keep all those little grains *entirely apart*, till the butter is thoroughly washed, and next, to bring it together after it is properly washed.

Now, there is only one thing that will keep the grains from adhering, and that is cold. Have the coldest water you can get, ice water in summer, and a handful or two of salt in it. Having drawn off your buttermilk, pour on enough of this cold brine to well cover the butter and then work the churn very slowly and gently for a minute, draw off the water, and put on some more, and, if necessary, repeat again, till the water runs off the butter as clear as when it was put on.

If properly managed, the butter will have been washed as if it were so much gravel or so much shot, and will not have adhered at all, but will lie in the churn, looking exactly like yellow wheat,—a bonny sight, and a profitable one as well.

In warm weather you may lift it out in that state, but in very cold weather it is better to pour on some more water at 62° to 65°, and let stand a few moments, then drain and take out on the worker. It will still be in grains, but not too hard to gather into a mass whenever you begin to work it.

Use only the very best salt, too much stress can hardly be laid upon that, and also *don't over-salt*. It won't keep the butter a bit better, but especially if the salt be the common poor stuff generally used, the butter will be actually bitter to the taste, and rough and gritty to the tongue. This is the poorest economy, and I think as much butter has been spoiled by this practice as by all other causes put together.

Use Ashton salt, or Higgins, or the nearest to those that you can get, and don't grudge the small extra cost, for it will pay you over and over again. If not as fine as it possibly can be made, sift it, and then stir it lightly and evenly into your granular butter, at the rate of half an ounce, three-quarters, or even a whole ounce to the pound, according to taste. But let me assure you that too much salt overpowers all the sweet and delicate flavor of your butter, and it is no longer the popular taste.

For packed butter (which, however, I never have to make) I would use an ounce to the pound; but for fresh or print butter, only half an ounce to the pound is my rule. I know this will surprise many, but try it and see how it works. The reputation my butter has got is a sufficient guarantee of its goodness, and lest anyone should think that I supply only a few people of peculiar taste, I may here state that, last year, the output of my dairy was seven thousand pounds.

Having thoroughly incorporated the salt, proceed to use the butter worker, but no more than is absolutely necessary to get the butter into a solid lump of even texture and color throughout. If it is not worked enough it will be streaky, but this is a thing that very seldom happens. One rarely sees butter hurt by too little working, while it is almost invariably spoiled by too much working.

Now, if the temperature of your dairy is just right, and can be kept that way, so the butter will neither get soft and oily, nor get hard and crumbly, you may, with advantage, leave it a couple of hours, to let the salt dissolve, and then make it up. But if you are not quite sure of this, finish it while you are about it, for you would lose more than you would gain by letting it stand.

Above all things, avoid the practice of some people of letting it stand all night. It is impossible to re-work it then without breaking the grain and greasing the butter.

If you print it, use a handsome print, with a good impression on top; not an elaborate device, which is seldom stamped perfectly, but one as simple as possible—a star, an acorn, or a sheaf of wheat. The best print I ever had I got in New York for forty cents, and it had a Scotch thistle on it; so deeply and clearly was the thistle cut in the wood, that the impression was just grand, as though carved in gold, and a hundred of those prints in rows, in an immense flat tin, filled with cold clear water before being packed, was a " sight for sair een " I can tell you.

# CHAPTER VIII.

## PRINTING.—PREPARING FOR MARKET.

I have said that I got my print in New York, and so I did, and it only cost me 40 cents, and lasted me for many years.

Its advantages were these : the clear, deep impression it made, the beautiful finish and smoothness of the wood, and above all the *straight sides.* If you want to succeed, look well to these small things.

I found the prints I got here were made of poor wood, and soon split; that the impression on top was cut in such a shallow way, and so roughly, that one could hardly tell what it was meant for; and also that the sides of print sloped *out,* towards the bottom, which looks very badly. On my New York print, the Scotch thistle on top stood up half an inch and more, and was the handsomest I ever saw; everyone exclaimed that they had never seen butter so beautifully printed. Besides which, straight sided prints pack better and closer, and don't bruise so much.

Better prints can now be had here, but there is still much to be desired in them. Square prints were once much in vogue, and I have used them a great deal, but I confess that I don't like their appearance so well.

The only advantages I can see are these, and they certainly count for a good deal: 1st.—You can pack these bricks of butter in a solid mass, and in much smaller space than any other form of print ; 2nd.— A good square print is so constructed that you can turn out *exactly* the weight required, 1 lb. or ½ lb. to each print, while with the round mould this is hardly possible.

Notwithstanding, I prefer the round one. You have got to please the people's eye, and if you are as expert at printing as you should be, you can soon come so close to the weight required as to surprise yourself.

And now let me caution you about one thing, *be sure and give full weight.* Whatever your prints are represented to weigh, see that they do so.

But, on the other hand, you must not rob yourself—this is more easily done than you would suppose, and these small leaks make a woeful difference in your balance sheet.

Perhaps I can best explain by relating my own actual experience :

I was working in my dairy, and I put on the scales a print which weighed half an ounce too much. A friend, who was watching me, said, " Oh, let it go at that, you won't lose much by it." I told her that the year before I had sent out 10,000 prints of butter. Had each one been half an ounce over weight that would mean at the end of the year 5000 ounces, or, in plain figures, a loss of $312\frac{1}{2}$ lbs. butter.

There is nothing like facts and figures in cases like this, and eternal vigilance is the price of success. Ask any milkman who sells milk out of cans, what proportion of loss there is in re-measuring, and I think you will be surprised.

Now, there must be some loss, but it is our own fault if that loss be excessive. We have no right to defraud ourselves to the extent that my friend suggested to me, for then liberality becomes wastefulness and justice degenerates into folly.

Yet, on the other hand, we *must* give good measure—we must give *down-weight, so that the scale will sink promptly, and no mistake about it.* Some loss there will certainly be, but if we are careful it will not be very great, and it will be amply covered by the entire satisfaction of our customers and the good price they are willing to pay, in consequence.

Now, as to wrapping up each print separately, it is most desirable,—in fact, it is really necessary, if you want to market your product in first-class shape. Unless in exceedingly cold weather, when it may be omitted, but I would not advise this even then.

I have not used any of the preparations of paper, though some are excellent and very cheap ; still, I prefer the cheese-cloth, not the unbleached, woolly stuff, that would not do at all, but the pure white cotton cheese bandage ; it is a yard wide, is free from dressing, and only costs about 6 cents a yard by the piece. Use this for all purposes about butter. Cut a number of squares, in evenings or odd times, and keep in a clean, dry place, and wrap each print in one, first wetting the cloth in cold water, lay the square on top of your print, and fold the four corners under the bottom. Then the tops of your prints will present a uniform and pleasing appearance, the yellow butter shining through the thin white cloth—and, besides, there is no danger of breaking the impression on top in detaching the corners of the cloth, when they are underneath.

Don't have your squares too big—they cost more, and look untidy.

In whatever case you lay your prints, be it basket, or wooden case, or drawer, let it be spotlessly clean and sweet and as new as possible. Have a square yard of the white cheese-cloth wrung out of ice water. Lay half of it smoothly in the bottom of basket or box. Arrange your prints neatly on it, each in its own white wrapping. Then fold the other half of your cloth over them, and over all lay a clean towel, fresh out of the folds.

And now, do not be angry if I give you one piece of advice:

Avoid, as you would poison, the bedroom towel, so often used for this purpose. You may say the towel is clean, and no doubt it is, but the *ideas it suggests* are not cleanly, and its use is enough to condemn the best basket of butter that ever went into market.

Still worse is the *old* piece of white cotton that has evidently seen years of service, and has then been torn off from something, one doesn't know what, and it is better not to enquire!

It will pay you over and again to have half a dozen or more large coarse, white linen towels, each marked " dairy " in large letters, and use them for nothing else. So much for preparing butter in prints.

If you can sell the whole lot to one person you suffer less loss than by selling in small lots. If you put it in rolls, there is less trouble and less loss, but, as a rule, it brings less money. If you prefer, however, to have it in rolls, whether of 5 lbs., 2 lbs., or 1 lb., see that they are all down-weight, and all so exactly alike that you can hardly tell one from the other. Let each one be neatly wrapped in a piece of wet white cheese-cloth, and laid evenly side by side.

Have your name plainly marked on all boxes, baskets and towels, and if you have strictly followed all my directions you will hardly be able to meet the demand for your butter. Your name will be a sufficient guarantee.

But don't expect this result all at once; that is an impossibility. Be patient and persevering, and you will succeed.

People who are regularly served with sweet, delicious yellow butter, all year round, in dainty and spotless packages, will not willingly do without it. They soon get to know that the full weight is always there, that the quality is always superlative, that the appearance is pleasing, and that the exquisite cleanliness is self-evident, and they will gladly pay more than the market price for it. But you must educate them up to this by degrees.

I have often heard visitors say : " Is this the famous Jersey butter ? It is very fine, but not so very wonderful after all.'' But, soon after, meeting these same people, they invariably exclaim : " You have spoiled us for any other butter ! We simply can't eat it now with any relish."

This is emphatically true.

Jersey butter steals into one's good graces before one knows it, and when it gets there it stays there. The same is true, to a certain extent, of all really good butter ; but once market an inferior lot, and your whole labor is undone, you have got to begin at the very beginning again, and handicapped with a damaged name at that.

# CHAPTER IX.

METHOD OF MARKETING PRINT BUTTER IN GILT EDGE DAIRIES.—
BEST BUTTER BOXES FOR SMALL LOTS, NOT PRINTED.

Print butter certainly brings a higher price than any other, and, if money alone be the object, it is well worth while to put it up in that form. But it often happens that there is not time for this, and the question arises, if I have to put up my butter in bulk, how shall I do it?

I have tried little crocks, and they are very nice, but they cost too much, and, besides, they are heavy to handle and liable to break.

I have tried neat white tubs lined with tin. These are a pretty package, but the tin soon rusts and corrodes from the salt. And, besides, no one who wants a fancy price for fancy butter wants to put it up in as large packages as these. It will, if of best quality, rank as A 1 tub butter, but it *will* be "tub butter," and this is not what we want.

We are now speaking of strictly fresh choice table butter—that which is most appropriately called, in the States, 10 days butter—meaning, that to be eaten in its prime it should all be consumed within 10 days of the time it is churned. And I will tell you how they manage this in the States.

The most delicious print butter is sent into the cities once a week, packed in Philadelphia ice tubs. In these the ice does not touch the butter, but is in a compartment by itself. This butter sells at from fifty cents to a dollar a pound, all through the week.

But (and here is the secret) at the end of the week, *every print remaining unsold is returned to the dairy from whence it came;* the dealer is credited with the amount returned, while a fresh made supply goes forward for the ensuing week.

The returned butter is sold in the neighborhood of the dairy for a fair price, but for nothing like city prices.

The wisdom of this policy must be apparent to every one. These dairymen hold their reputation above everything else, and jealously guard it. Nothing would induce them to allow one print of their butter to go on the market that was not churned within the week, and that was not strictly up to their usual standard. They would not sell a print of butter that had begun to "go off" even if they were offered ten dollars a pound for it, because the ten dollars *in* their pocket to-day would be many hundreds of dollars *out of it* in the future, and they are keenly alive to this fact.

As a result, a customer once got is never lost, and even a fall in prices does not affect them. People *know* that the name of such a firm is like the Hall mark on silver, or the stamp on a guinea, that it is a warranty of absolute perfection in that line, and then the public have got to have these goods, and won't be satisfied with any other.

If people could only be brought to realize this, and to act upon it, what a revolution it would make in business! "Honesty is the best policy," is quoted glibly enough, and often by those who don't even know what honesty means; but let me tell you that under that trite old saying there is a meaning as deep as the sea and as wide as the world, if people would only see it.

You will say, "what of the loss involved by butter returned to the dairy and sold at a reduced price?"

There is no loss.

In the first place, there is but little returned, so great is the demand. Often, for weeks together, there is none at all returned, as supply has been short.

In the second place, even this returned butter is sold at a price that would seem wonderful to many a farmer, and at a price that pays well for its making. Neighbors all round know exactly what it is, and are only too glad to get it. They use it immediately, as they are supposed to do, and are well pleased. The dairies make a good profit on this returned butter, and what they make on the higher-priced city butter is just so much more clear profit over and above that again.

This is a most satisfactory state of things, but it can only be attained by adhering *rigidly* to the fixed rules laid down. Once yield to temptation for the sake of present gain, and your reputation is gone, and can never be regained.

A great trouble with us is that we are short-sighted, narrow, greedy and grasping.

We are not content to build up a reputation by slow degrees, knowing that people will soon awake to the fact that they can't do without us, and *must* pay our price. We want to charge the price right away, and then convince the people afterwards how superior our goods are.

Now, this is all wrong—it is the cart before the horse.

If you want to succeed, *convince people first* and then charge them afterwards.

Now, I will tell you how I put up a great deal of my butter. From S. J. White, of Belleville, I get small round boxes, hooped with tin, and paraffined inside. These come in "nests," if desired, are exceedingly neat and attractive, clean, strong enough for all practical purposes, and wonderfully light to handle. The most desirable sizes hold 3 lbs., 5 lbs., 7 lbs., and 10 lbs. each.

They are also in general use in the States.

Fill a few of these boxes with sweet, yellow, fragrant butter, and pack with dainty care, not smearing the edges. Lay a round of white " cheese-cloth " wrung out of cold water on top, sprinkle on a little fine salt, cover tightly, and stencil your name on it, and then see if your work does not do you credit.

These little boxes are to be packed in outer cases of any size desired, but *even these* I prefer to have of dressed stuff, neat and tidy. Of course, these boxes are not returned, but you do not expect it, as the cost is trifling. A 10 lb. box costs 10 cents, and an outer case holding six of these boxes (60 lbs.) costs 10 cents more.

And I don't know of any other way in which 60 lbs. of fresh table butter can be put up, in faultless and most attractive style, at a cost of 70 cents.

# CHAPTER X.

## ON CHURNS.

I have often been asked what kind of churn, butterworker, etc., I use. I use a Bullard churn, made in the States.

I do not say that it is the *best* churn in the world, because I don't think so, but I do say that there is no better.

I got it in this way: My husband was visiting one of the greatest Jersey breeders in the States, many years ago, and was so delighted with the butter there that he took note of all the dairy fixtures, and got me duplicates, whenever he could.

The Bullard churn is simply an oblong box (straight sides and ends) with a cover on the top, about a foot square. This cover, when fitted on, is secured by two buttons. From a stout, oblong frame, on the floor, rise two uprights, or legs, about 2 by 10 and 3 ft. high. These stand cross-ways of the frame, about three feet apart, and on them rests a stout board, 3 feet long and 10 inches wide. These legs, or uprights, are pinned to this platform, as well as to the frame below, so that they can be pushed to and fro.

On the bottom of the churn are four cleats, along the four edges, so when the churn is lifted on the platform it just fits down upon it and does not slide off. By a round wooden roller, reaching across one end of the churn box, it is firmly held by a man, and pushed from him and drawn towards him at any speed desired.

There are wheels with the churn, so that it may be attached to steam or any other power, but, of late years, we work it by hand.

Formerly, I tried a power, but either *we* were not a success or the power was not. Objecting to have any animal on a tread power, I got a small sweep, but it was made by one of those geniuses found in most country neighborhoods, who are cheap to begin with but ruinous in the end.

And what a time we did have with it, to be sure!

There was no horse on the place that was *always* at our disposal but the children's pony, and how she did hate and despise that churning power! If left to herself, she would walk slower and slower, till at last she would actually stop, and I do believe she was asleep half the time. Then, when she was vigorously awakened, she would start with a jump, till the churn nearly flew through the dairy roof.

As a result, it took two people,—one to mind the pony, and one to mind the churn.

We then tried a large gray mare, that went rather better; but one day a little boy who was visiting at our house threw a stone at gray Lucy as she was going around, and nearly frightened her to death. She bolted and jumped over a fence, taking part of the power with her, and as it was pretty well worn out we never got it repaired.

We churn 30 lbs. at a time. The foreman can do it alone, and sometimes does, but it is a heavy business, and so, as a rule, when all is ready to begin, his assistant comes in and helps at the other end of the churn, till the butter comes, and hardly misses the time.

In the Bullard churn are no dashers of any kind whatever—simply the box, and nothing more. There is a ventilator at the top, and a place at one end for drawing off the buttermilk. It is simple, durable, and easily cleaned. I don't see how it could be improved upon.

But there are great numbers of capital churns in our Canadian markets,—in fact, the difficulty is to find a poor one.

I have also used, with much satisfaction, the Davis Swing churn. I think it works easier than any I know. Especially is this true of a *tin* churn that has a round body while the ends are conical. This is, in a minute, hooked on to two chains, which hang from the ceiling, and a delicate woman, by having the chains long enough, can sit down in her chair, and work the churn with the greatest ease and comfort, pushing it from her and then pulling on the string attached to the end.

I know this may sound absurd to some who find it difficult to get out of the old rut, but just let them try it and they will be surprised and delighted. At any rate, anything is worth trying that will lighten the labor of the over-tasked wife and mother.

I say plainly, and without hesitation, that a heavy churning in an old-fashioned dash churn is not fit work for any woman, be she ever so strong.

Of course, I don't allude to the 3 or 4 lbs. of butter sometimes churned for table use by the thrifty housewife, with pride and pleasure, but to extensive dairy work, which is not only far too heavy, but, from the peculiar motion involved, is most injurious to all females.

These tin churns are easier kept clean and sweet than wooden ones, and are far lighter to lift and carry. For those whose churnings are not too large, I cordially recommend them.

The Blanchard churn is also a good one. All those I have seen have revolving dashers, but they make capital butter. However, turning the crank is, to me, more laborious than any other way of churning, while some people think it easier. But if an able-bodied man does that part of the work (as he should do) I don't think he will be found particular as to the motion. If all be ready when he comes in, and cream properly tempered, so he is not kept churning for hours, he will generally be pretty good-natured over it, and soon bring the butter.

Barrel churns I don't like quite so well, because if they *do* leak, they make a slop on the floor. And nothing makes such a mess as milk, unless it is quickly and thoroughly cleaned up. In factories or large dairies where the floor is often of cement, and there is every convenience for flushing it with lots of water, it is all very well, and the barrel churn has the advantage of holding more than any other. But in a dairy like mine, being only one of my house cellars, I prefer the Bullard churn, or one similar to it, because I find it the most convenient.

A good churn is a good thing, and it is highly important to have one that is easily cleaned. But it doesn't do to pin your faith entirely to the churn, for good and bad butter can be made in the same one.

But *not* by the same person.

I may now state that I never have made better butter than I did 16 years ago, when I first got my Jersey cows. I had been in the habit of churning, or having churned, enough butter for table use, many years before that, and had learned all I could about the best methods. And when I first got Jerseys I kept an accurate account of everything, and have done so ever since. I found that, at the end of 12 months, I made 2500 lbs. of as fine butter as I ever saw or tasted, and it was all churned in an old-fashioned dash churn, and worked with a wooden bowl and ladle.

I do not recommend this, as it is too laborious, but I only mention it to show what can be done, even under adverse circumstances.

## CHAPTER XI.

As for butter-workers, I am sorry I can't recommend those of Canadian make as I do the churns. I have never seen but one that, to my mind, is thoroughly satisfactory, and that is Reid's, made in the States (sometimes called the Philadelphia).

It is an oblong wooden tray, over which a corrugated roller passes to and fro, being worked by a crank. Mine cost eight dollars, besides duty and freight, and I would not take $100 for it if I could not get another. The tray is made of the best well seasoned white wood, and the cogs and travellers are of galvanized iron. I never saw anything that, in my opinion, worked butter so thoroughly and easily, and yet preserved the grain so well, and they are so splendidly made as to last for many years. I have only had two in 16 years, and, as I work now about 7000 lbs. of butter a year, the durability of these articles is apparent.

Lest I may be accused of injustice to my own country (although I sincerely hope not), I may state that I was greatly delighted, some years ago, to find that a company in a town near us were making the Reid butter-worker. As I was then in want of a new one, I was only too glad to give them the order, and when the article came home, it looked precisely like the one I had got from Philadelphia years before.

But when I came to use it, I soon saw the difference.

In spite of everyday use, the seams opened and the wood warped. The castings also were poor, and in a short time the whole thing went to pieces, and was broken up for kindling.

It does seem a pity that some firms cannot be found enterprising enough to make a first-class article of this pattern ; they would sell by thousands.

If I had not a Reid, I should use the common three-cornered one standing on three legs, and worked by a roller, one end of which fits into a socket in the angle, while the other is held in the hand, and pressed down upon the butter. But this is more tiresome to me.

For anything which I can't get in Canada I send to the Vermont Farm Machine Co., of Bellows Falls, Vermont, U.S. It has been said that what this Company have not got is not worth having, and there is a deal of truth in the remark.

Some people have asked me if I use sugar or saltpetre in my butter. I answer no, nothing whatever but a very small allowance of the very best salt that money can buy.

Next to dirt poor salt spoils more butter than anything else. I have eaten butter, and so have we all, in which hard crystals of undissolved salt gritted between the teeth, and the taste was nearly as bitter as though *Epsom* salts had been used.

As to sugar, etc., the very largest quantity you could dare to use is too small, by far, to be any help towards keeping the butter, while if your churning is good, these things won't improve it, and if it is poor, they won't redeem it.

Many people believe in putting as much foreign stuff as they can into butter, and also in leaving as much water as they dare in it, because it then weighs heavier, and salt, sugar and water all cost less by the pound than good butter. But rest assured that this is the wrong way to work.

I am not speaking in the interest of the purchaser, but in your own interest. If you want an extra price you have *got to* make an extra article, and to stick to it.

If a man says "there is a roll of butter, and I want 15 cents a lb· for it," a purchaser can take it or leave it, just as he chooses, and if he finds it oozing with water and bitter with bad salt, he cannot reasonably complain. The farmer did not profess to make extra butter, nor did he ask the price of a prime article.

But let a man offer good looking butter, and claim that it is as nearly perfect as butter ever gets to be, and let him ask and get 35 cents per lb. for it, and then see how quickly he will hear from his customers if it is not up to the mark, and how they will steer clear of him another time.

If, through any misfortune or accident, you have a poor churning, don't put it upon your customers or upon the market at all as good butter. Sell it, representing it exactly as what it is—an off-churning—to some confectioner, who habitually uses that class of butter.

If you can't do that and can't eat it at home (and of course you can't if you have been in the habit of eating good butter), then use it for axle grease, as unfit for food. This will be no loss, but money in your pocket in the end.

The loss was in *making* the bad butter, and not in throwing it away. If you have had the ill luck, or rather the carelessness, to make poor butter, don't throw good money after bad by trying to sell it, and spoiling your name; that is only making a bad business worse.

To return to working butter. There are thousands of women to-day in Canada, who, to the shame of their husbands be it spoken, have no sort of butter-worker at all, but use the bowl and ladle.

I fancy I can see them, especially when the weather is getting cold and butter hardens almost immediately.

The butter breaks into small crumbs the minute the cold water touches it, till the whole thing looks like barley broth more than anything else, and the poor woman chases these particles around the bowl, pressing and patting and coaxing them together, and just as she gets one portion of it solid, or thinks she does, another part breaks away, and she is in as bad a mess as ever, and strength and patience both give out.

Oh yes, I know all about it, for I've been there myself many a time and know how it feels.

But there is no need for this, if we only go the right way to work. And in my next chapter I will tell what I found to be the best way out of the scrape.

# CHAPTER XII.

EASE AND COMFORT IN CHURNING.—BUTTER COLOR.—" BIG LITTLE
THINGS " IN THE DAIRY.—THE MAN WHO FOLLOWS HIS
GRANDMOTHER.

The best way out of the scrape referred to in my last chapter is *to buy* a thermometer, and to see that it is used.

Then there will be no more weary churning for hours and hours, no more frothing cream or hard, white crumbly butter, no aching back or arms over a wretched, greasy little lump that is not fit to be called butter.

If your cream has been properly kept all along, and properly ripened, and if it has been brought to a proper temperature, 24 hours before churning, *and held at that*, you should have no more trouble than you would with June butter.

Next, as to washing. Don't dash icy water on to your butter in winter, and then wonder that, at the last, it won't adhere.

I may have said this before, but I can't say it too often; wash with water just cold enough to *keep the particles from adhering*, till every trace of milk is removed, and water runs off as clear as crystal, and then submerge in water a little bit warmer, according to the season, and gently churn for a few seconds—not enough to unite the butter, you don't want that just yet, but enough for it to take, from the tempered water, the waxy, yet yielding consistency of summer butter. Lift it out, still in granules or grains, or, if preferred, stir the salt into it, in the churn, but thoroughly and evenly mix it through the wheatlike mass, and do it quickly for fear the butter gets too hard again, and then pass your roller over it, or work with ladle (if you have to do that), and you will find it unite quickly and easily into a compact, yellow mass, that it is a pleasure to handle.

And this is why I advocate working butter only once. So few have the facilities for keeping it at just the right temperature during the interval, and so few have judgment enough to avoid over-working it the second time.

Right here, let me answer a question that has been asked me hundreds of times, viz., What butter color do I use ?

Naturally, when I can avoid it I don't use any.

But sometimes it is absolutely necessary to do so, if we wish to please the taste of our customers and, I may add, our own eye also.

My cows are especially noted for the deep yellow color of their butter, and I have often, in summer, been requested to use less coloring, when as a matter of fact I was not using any at all !

But let people talk as they like, *no* cow will make as yellow butter in January as she will in June, and especially is that the case if you avoid (as I do) the feeding of much cornmeal.

But people want their fresh butter exactly the same color all the year round, and *will have it so ;* therefore, when I have to add coloring, I get none but that made by Wells, Richardson & Co. Again and again I have been begged to try other preparations, and have done so (as it seems unfair to refuse), but *in no* case have I found anything that can *at all* compare with that made by Wells, Richardson & Co., and, in my opinion, it leaves nothing to be desired. It is simply the perfection of June color, and makes one think of new-mown hay and roses and all sorts of summery things.

And my opinion of this (as also of *all* articles or utensils referred to in this book) is *entirely* unsolicited. I simply try to tell the best things to use, as well as the best way to make butter.

But, to return to our churning.

If, from any cause, the lump of butter has to be left in the bowl till it is as hard as a stone, don't set it near the stove, as is commonly done, or you will certainly spoil it. The side next the fire will become so soft and oily as to spoil the whole churning, while the inside of the lump will remain as hard as a rock.

Cut your butter into pieces, not bigger than your fist, and drop into a pail of water tempered to from 62° to 65°, and keep the water at that heat, putting a plate or some such thing over the butter to keep it down. After a while you will find it more evenly softened throughout than in any other way, and you can work it with comparative ease.

If you have a large quantity to print, and have to do it in a very cold cellar, it is a good plan to immerse the bulk of the butter in this way, and only take off a pound or two at a time.

Lots of people will tell you that they can do just as well without a thermometer, and that they can tell the exact temperature of water with their hand.

*They can't do it* at all times, or with any degree of certainty at all. If you have been out doors, and come in with hands half frozen, even a very cold pail of water will seem warm to them, and *vice versa*. And even if, by dint of skill and guess-work, they do manage the churning fairly well five or six times, they will be certain to miss it before long, and then, as I said before, hours of weary work in the dairy follow, heaps of other work left undone in the meantime, weary limbs, angry temper, poor butter at last, and discomfort and misery all through.

And all this can be avoided by the use of a thermometer, which costs 30 cents, and the use of a little common sense, which costs nothing at all.

It is worth remembering, however, that thick, rich cream from well-fed cows is more quickly and easily churned than the thin, white stuff, half milk, from half-starved cattle.

A word about your thermometer. Don't tie a string to it to sink it in the cream, for it soon becomes foul and ill-smelling. Fasten a slender flexible wire to it. This is better than a string, and is easily kept clean and sweet.

When I had to work butter in a bowl, and, indeed, very often since then, I will tell you what I found a great help and comfort. A large, clean, common sponge, tied up like a dumpling, in a square of white cheese cloth. Wring this dumpling tightly out of clean, cool water, and with it dab over the surface of your butter and take up the water that accumulates in bottom of bowl. This convenience costs but a few cents, and you have no idea what a help and comfort it is till you try it! Of course, you dip the sponge in the water, or squeeze dry again every few minutes, but you do your work in half the time, and twice as well. It is one of the "big little things" of the dairy.

Do not think it tedious to attend to all these things. One bad day in the dairy is far more tedious than attending to all the rules that ever were written. It is true that, under some circumstances, and at certain seasons of the year, butter will almost make itself, but these are the exceptions.

At such times the ignorant and obstinate crow loudly and long.

*They* need no thermometer, and no book learning; *they* don't work by rule of thumb, but just guess at it, like their mothers and grandmothers did before them.

Forgetting that, in those old times (which seem at a distance so much better than they really were), winter dairying was a thing almost unknown.

Forgetting, too, that our worthy ancestors were, like ourselves, more prone to proclaim from the housetops their successes than their failures, and so, when they came to grief, we were not very apt to hear about it, or to remember it if we did hear.

Just wait till the weather gets frosty and changeable, till the cows shrink in their milk, and get too much frozen grass, and too little grain and warm mashes, and then call on these good "guessers," and see how things are going with them.

If it is a woman who is struggling in the dairy, where everything is going wrong from beginning to end, you will feel so sorry for her you won't know what to say, and can only wonder at her patience, and feel that it is worthy of a better cause.

But if it is a man that is working there, better not go in, for you can see enough of the circus without.

From the dairy door issues the steam of the boiling tea-kettle and sounds of profanity, together with calls upon every female on the place to wait upon him, and to bring him lots more hot water, and not to stand there gaping like fools, and he tells them that "churning is woman's work, anyhow."

But not one word about his grandmother!

Oh no, not to-day.

And when, at last, the bitter and unprofitable end is reached, he slams the churn, and kicks a pail over, and leaving the dairy in a hopeless mess goes out and kicks the cow, and then goes round that place like a comet for the rest of the day.

# CHAPTER XIII.

### AN ANSWER TO MR. DOHERTY.—PRACTICAL EXPERIENCE.

I had got thus far in my labors when I was very ably criticized by a gentleman who writes :—" In my previous investigations I was led to believe that an animal of 1000 lbs. weight required 21 lbs. of digestible dry matter per day, consisting of 2.50 albuminoids, 12.50 carbo-hydrates and 40 fat. Now, Mrs. Jones, during the months of November, December and January, fed her cow 31.35 lbs. of digestible dry matter made up of 3.13 albuminoids, 19.06 carbo-hydrates and .94 fat, which, according to my previous teaching, should be sufficient for a cow weighing 1635 lbs., or about enough for two medium-sized cows of 800 lbs. each. Without giving us seekers after truth any reason for the same, Mrs. Jones, during the months of February, March and April, drops the ration one-half to the same cow, and feeds 17.62 lbs. digestible dry matter, composed of 1.61 albuminoids, 9.76 carbo-hydrates and .51 fat, which, with the exception of .19 fat in excess and a deficiency of .39 in albuminoids, appears to be a pretty well balanced ration for a cow of 800 lbs. The fact of her cow giving four-fifths as much butter during these last months (although progressing toward time of calving) as during the previous ones, leads me to suspect that about one-half of the food eaten during the earlier months was not assimilated, but thrown off with the other excretions, or else the cow was an excessively large Holstein, weighing at least 1635 lbs. Still, the fact remains unexplained why the change of feed was made in February. I, like Mrs. Jones, believe in generous feeding ; at the same time I should like to be rational in my method. I would not consider it reasonable to feed a cow more than she would digest and assimilate, nor would I think of cutting down her ration one-half without a sufficient cause."

(Signed),      J. H. DOHERTY.

Now, my whole aim and object is to elicit just such remarks, to invite criticism, to compare notes with my neighbors, and by our united efforts to find out what we are all striving to learn, viz., what is the truth.

And we will never arrive at the truth, till we discard all ignorance and prejudice, all conceit and self-sufficiency, and all narrow-mindedness ; till we are ready and willing to learn, open to conviction, and quick to acknowledge our mistakes.

And we will never achieve a national success in dairying, or in anything else, till we unite in making a long pull, a strong pull, and a pull all together.

To return to our cow. She was not a Holstein, but a cross between Jersey and Ayrshire, a remarkably large animal of her kind, with a wonderful appetite and a great constitution, but she did not weigh 1000 lbs.

Mr. Doherty thinks that at one time I over-fed this cow, thereby incurring loss and waste, while later on she was getting less than he thinks needful of digestible, dry matter. I will try to explain why I disagree with him. 1st. Mr. Doherty was misled by a misprint which appeared in the paper that published the test of the cow referred to in Chap. 3. It gave quantity of hay as only 8 lbs. a day, just half of the cow's previous ration, whereas, had Mr. D. looked at *the price* as carried out, he would have at once detected the misprint, and would have seen that the cow was getting 16 lbs. hay a day, the same as before. It was only her grain ration that was cut down nearly half, and as to that, I would say it is absolutely impossible to lay down any exact ration that will apply equally well to all milk cows, just as it is impossible to portion out an exact quantity of food, and have it exactly the right thing for all human beings. What would be insufficient for one person would satiate another, and *vice versa*, and it is just the same with animals. Consequently, when we give a ration, we simply give it *as a basis*, upon which the intelligent farmer works with considerable variation, according to circumstances.

Take the accounts of many of the first milk and butter dairies, both in Europe and America, and read the quantity of food given, in equal measure, to all cows.

But what follows?

These authorities say : "If any cow then looks for more, give her more, and if any cow has left a portion of her feed, take it at once away from her."

No words could show more plainly the wide variation in the appetite and requirements of different animals of the same species.

These large establishments, it is safe to assume, are, for the most part, run in the most economical manner and so as to obtain the very best results, and they feed most liberally.

I have one fixed belief which nothing can alter, and that is that so long as the food is not too rich or concentrated, a milking cow should have *all she will eat*, except for the 3 months previous to calving. (And, even then, it is quite possible that I err in reducing the feed too much, but I am so afraid of milk fever that I prefer to err, if at all, on the safe side.)

Take a lot of cows in pasture. Some are soon satisfied and lie down, while others continue eating, as though they could never get enough.

We don't go out to the pasture with a scientific book in one hand, and stop those cows from eating, and tell them they have had enough —so much digestible matter, so much starch, and so much fat, etc., and that, if they are not satisfied, they ought to be, and have got to quit.

Not at all. We recognize that the cow is the best judge in the pasture, and, to a great extent, I think she should be the best judge in the stable, too, if we are reasonably careful as to what her ration is composed of.

2. Immediate results are not obtained from any one mode of feeding. Mr. Doherty wonders that my cow continued to make so large a quantity of butter upon so much less food than she had previously been getting.

In answer, I would say, the cow could not have done so had she not been so well fed for months before. She was drawing on the reserve she had in store, and which every cow should have.

The best authorities, and those who have made the largest yearly tests, claim that we should feed a cow to her highest working capacity for a whole year before expecting a great test, and they prove that the effects of good food are far more lasting than most people are at all aware of.

3. When I give the alterations in my rations, I don't wish to be understood as making those changes suddenly—that would be a crazy thing to do. If I say that during 3 months I feed a cow 15 lbs. of

grain a day, I don't mean that she eats exactly that quantity every day of the 3 months; not at all. I mean that she averages that quantity, eating more than that at first and less than that at the last, and so, reducing her feed gradually, avoiding sudden changes as in the case of this cow.

No one is infallible, and few, indeed, can hit the happy medium exactly. But I honestly think that I fed the cow to good advantage, and that her yield proved it. If we over-feed a cow we are seldom left long in the dark about it, for in most cases the animal soon shows it, either by a fit of indigestion or by getting too fat. Then the careful owner will be warned at once and change his ways.

My cattle have been extensively exhibited through the province, and I have never yet heard them called too fat or over-fed.

4. Although, as I say, I used my best judgment in feeding my cow—although she was as sleek and fine as silk, the very pink of health, not the least too fat, and yielded immensely and no waste in her droppings that I could detect, yet in spite of all this I may be wrong; there may have been waste, although I did not and still do not think so.

Far be it from me to set up as infallible. If I am mistaken I am heartily glad to have it pointed out, and, as I said previously, it is quite possible that the public may learn far more from my many failures than they will ever learn from my modest successes.

I don't ask people to follow me, I ask them to *come with me*. I am eager to ask all that they know, and eager, also, to tell them all that I know, so we may help each other.

With every regard for science, I may yet say that there is danger of carrying it to extremes, and that many able articles on dairying are away above the people's heads. Anyway, they are above my head, that much I am sure of.

If I want to try a cow, I don't send her milk to be analyzed; though, no doubt, that is good. But I set her milk and churn it, and then I work the butter properly till it is as firm nearly as wax and as sweet as a rose, so that I may claim quality as well as quantity.

Give me the scales and weights and good common sense every time.

And if it is not too egotistical, let me here say that I have never been able to devote myself exclusively to dairying; far from it.

The care and nursing and teaching of my children, the sewing, housekeeping and social calls, and all the many duties of a house mother have claimed my time as well, so I have not been able to make exhaustive scientific experiments, but I have kept my eyes open and have done my best.

All my methods have been essentially those of the farmers around me—no costly devices, but all for utility and economy.

I am not talking down from a height (which farmers hate), I am standing on the same level with them, right side by side.

While I do not habitually work in my dairy now, yet I have done so to a great extent, and there is not one single process from milking and feeding my cow to churning the butter and making it up and washing the pails that I have not often done myself.

Why, in one year I churned, worked, printed and shipped to New York ten thousand prints of butter all with my own hands; no one else touched it.

I may not be able to analyze a pail of milk or a bucket of feed, but I can make a pound of good butter. I may not be able to feed a cow in the most correct scientific way, but there is one thing that I most certainly can do, I can feed her so she will pay.

## CHAPTER XIV.

### ON THE CARE OF DAIRY UTENSILS.

So much has been said and written on the subject of cleanliness in the Dairy, that anything from me may be thought superfluous—yet, a very few words may not be out of place in reference to some of my own mistakes.

When I first had the care of milk pans and pails, I prided myself upon the thorough scaldings I gave them, and thought no one could be cleaner than I was.

Imagine my mortification when my tins soon lost their brightness, and did not even look clean ! Worse still, a thick yellow coating came over them that I thought I would *never* get off, especially if there was a dinge or bruise in the pail, making an uneven surface.

I was in despair. I knew I spent more time and trouble upon my tins than most people, and yet I was ashamed to have them seen.

At last I unburdened my mind to a dear old lady, and how she did laugh at me, to be sure !

" Why, child," she said, "you have *cooked* the milk on to the sides of your tins by pouring in boiling water, and you will find it harder to get off than the bark off a tree."

And it certainly was.

But I did get it off at last, and then was most careful to do as my friend told me—only to use *lukewarm* suds, at first, till all milk and butter were thoroughly removed from pans, pails, churn and butter-worker, etc. ; then to rinse in clean warm water, and *then* to bring on my cherished tea-kettle, and scald all I wanted to, and the more the better.

Since then I have had no trouble when doing it myself, but the difficulty is to get hired girls into the right way and to keep them there.

I remember one that I had who wanted two dozen more kitchen towels. I thought I had a large enough supply, till I found that she was faithfully washing and *drying* every pan and pail used in our large dairy, as though they were so many cups and saucers.

She was quite surprised when I told her that tins would *dry themselves* if scalded with water that was actually boiling.

I showed her my method when I had 30 or 40 shallow pans to scald. After they were *well* cleaned, I turned one upside down on the platform of sink, and scalded the bottom, and then turned it up again, and put about two quarts boiling water in it, and then put another pan inside that, and two quarts water in it, and so on, till I had a pile as high as convenient. As each pan settled down with weight of the others above it, the water rose and flowed over the edges of the under ones, so *every part of every pan* got well scalded, and the whole pile was smoking and steaming. The top one I filled to overflowing, and then, after a few minutes, I took them all down, and laid them in rows on the benches.

Some people just put them in piles, but I never do this, as they don't dry, but just sweat, and get cold and clammy.

I turn the first pan upside down on the bench, taking care to let it *project over the end* a little, so the air can get inside. Then lean the next pan on it, resting partly on the first pan and partly on the bench, so it is on a slant, and then another and another, till all are done.

In this way they dry at once, and are thoroughly aired, and as sweet and clean as new tins.

Nor do I ever turn a pail or can upside down, so the air cannot enter, or *cover* a churn or any similar vessel.

Abundance of *scalding hot* water and then lots of air and sunshine, will tell the tale in the butter beyond mistake.

Of course, *wooden* things must not be left out in the sun too much till they warp and crack ; a little care will prevent this.

Butter will stick like tar to woodenware that is not properly taken care of, and I know of few things more annoying.

There is no remedy but to begin again. Thoroughly wash your print, or butter-worker, or whatever it is, being careful to get every particle of grease away. Then *thoroughly* scald, using plenty of water, and rub *well* with salt. Next, plunge into cold water and leave to soak for a while, and you will find all go well.

If you have a print not in frequent use, it is a good plan to wash and scald it every few days, just as though you were *going to* use it. This will keep the wood from cracking and leave the print in nice order.

The churn and everything in and about the Dairy should be cleansed *at once* after they are used.

It is nearly impossible to get things sweet and clean if they are left for hours, or perhaps all night, with sour cream or buttermilk or melting butter on them, to be absorbed by the wood, so it will never seem the same again.

The floor should be often and well washed, for milk, so sweet and wholesome when fresh, soon becomes one of the foulest things in creation, so quickly does it decompose.

I once went to a picnic when I was young, and took a stone jar of milk just drawn from the cow, corking the jar tightly.

We were delayed in reaching the island, and did not have tea till eight o'clock, but, on uncorking my jar of milk the odor was so strong that I threw it all away.

Fortunately, some one else had brought milk, so mine was not missed, but it taught me a lesson.

To many of my readers this is only the old, old story, but there are always beginners who are glad of such hints.

I know that in my young days I would have been pleased indeed to have had instruction from some one who really knew how—who had *actually done the work themselves.*

But nearly everything I know has been learnt by hard experience, and often by repeated and discouraging failures.

There are no truer words than those written by Marion Harland, in her Cookery Book. She says the most important thing is " to learn how *not* to do it."

And in no place is that more true than in the Dairy.

# CHAPTER XV.

## HOW I KEEP MY CATTLE.

I keep them under such difficulties as I hope few people have to contend with.

We own our house, with a few acres of land, just barely outside the limits of a very large and thriving town.

Our own land is poor enough, but that around us is still worse, being sometimes underlaid with rock for whole acres together, and all of it badly run down.

Not wishing to part with our home, we had just to do the best we could, and have rented two small farms, in rear of us, of 45 and 65 acres respectively.

Not only have we to go nearly half a mile to get to these farms, but we have also to cross the railway track to do so, and what with poor land and poor fences, or rather no fences at all, it is uphill work.

The walk is too far for both the cows and the men who drive them, nor is it possible for me to be out there as much as I ought.

Were the land under my own eye, things would do better, but with conflicting duties and heavy household cares, I have just got to get along as best I can. The cattle barns, however, are on our own place, just adjoining the horse stable, so that everything about *them* is under my own supervision.

We have a very large barn or stable, capable of holding 30 milking cows, and having two roomy loose boxes.

The cows stand facing each other, and have a 6-foot alley between their heads, this alley being of cement.

Each cow has a stall to herself, so there is no crowding or fighting. In rear of each row of cows is the gutter, and behind that again a board walk about 3 feet wide.

Just in the middle of the stable a broad cement passage runs *across*, intersecting the rows of cows, so there are, really, four rows of stalls.

There are large doors at the end of this cross alley, where the cows come in and turn to right or left, as the case may be, each cow knowing her own place.

After trying many fastenings, and finding most of them good, but needing a deal of bedding, and *then* not keeping the cows clean without more labor than I could afford, I heard of the stanchion made by Mr. Warriner, of Forestville, Conn.

These I put in last fall, and the longer I have them the more I like them. I have never seen anything that gives as much freedom and comfort to the animals consistent with cleanliness, and have pleasure in cordially recommending them.

In the cross alley is the bench for setting the milk pails on. To me it has always seemed a disgusting practice to set the milk pails on the floor behind the cows, and I have never allowed it.

Beside the bench is a high but small desk, the lid of which lifts up, and here the foreman can write and keep his papers. Under the desk is a small cupboard where many useful things are kept, a jar of linseed oil, a bottle of castor oil, one of laudanum, one of aromatic ammonia, one of turpentine, and one of carbolic oil. Some ginger and some epsom salts complete the list of simple remedies kept on hand, and with them and that blessed " ounce of prevention " that means so much, the herd is kept in splendid health. In one end of this barn are the root house and the silo. Above the root house is the feed room, reached by a short flight of steps, and furnished with great bins; and back of this is the engine room, with a good steam engine. At one time we kept the engine running all winter to cut and steam feed, pulp roots, grind oats, etc., but for many reasons I discontinued this, and we now use the engine only in fall to cut the corn for the silo.

Another barn is used for the bulls, of which we keep three, each in a large, loose box.

There is also a place for two yearling bulls (when we have them), and all the south side of the building is divided into little calf pens.

I find this a much better arrangement for the little creatures than being in the cow barn, as it is more easily kept at an even temperature.

In the large barn when the doors are opened and thirty cows let out to drink or exercise, the temperature falls so much as to chill young calves, besides which the cows are quieter and more content when the little ones are entirely away from them.

In a third and smaller barn there is room for 6 or 7 cows or heifers, besides two more loose boxes.

Everything is of the *very plainest* description. I have nothing that the poorest farmer cannot have, unless it be the steam engine, and many of them have got that.

Also, the gas that lights the large barn and engine room. We make this ourselves to light the house, and as a matter of safety and convenience had it put in the barn.

These buildings form three sides of a yard, that has a good well in the centre and a long water trough.

Adjoining the yard are two or three paddocks, where calves can be kept, also cows that are near calving.

In winter the stalls are cleaned out at 5 a.m., and cows brushed off, and each one receives a feed of ensilage with the proper quantity of meal and bran mixed with it, according to the milk they are giving. They are then milked, each gets an armful of hay, and the hands go to breakfast. Next, all animals are well carded and cleaned, all manure wheeled out of the stable, and calf pens and loose boxes thoroughly cleaned out.

Towards noon cattle are let out to water. If it be mild and fine, they remain out from one to three hours, according to the weather, but *never* till they get chilled. On returning to the stable each animal finds a feed of sliced roots in the box with a handful of meal or bran sprinkled on.

At four o'clock they are all offered water in pails, then they receive their second feed of ensilage and meal.

At five p.m. milking begins, after which each cow receives a liberal feed of hay and fresh bedding, and is then left for the night.

In summer, cows are milked at same time in morning, and cleaned. Each milking animal receives a quart of bran and of ground oats, as the pasture happens to be good or poor.

If the grass is very poor, all receive a good allowance of green fodder, either lucerne, green oats, peas, or corn fodder. They are then driven to pasture, returning before five o'clock, when they get the same feed (if any be necessary), and, after milking, are taken back to the pasture for the night.

Salt is given them as they wish, and blows, kicks, or rough words are unknown to them.

A couple of grade Ayrshires are generally kept to feed the calves, their milk is not so rich, and calves seem to do better on it.

Much of our land being in pasture, we do not grow all the feed we need, but buy largely.

We generally have 15 to 18 acres of corn, which gives us green feed for summer, fills the silo, and leaves us quite an amount of dry corn fodder, stooked, which lasts till near Christmas.

We also grow two to three thousand bushels of roots (mangels and carrots), 800 to 1000 bushels of oats, and potatoes enough for family use, besides 20 to 40 tons of hay.

We have always a patch of lucerne and one of peas and oats to feed green.

Fortunately, there is an 8 acre field adjoining our property which we rent, and here abide the lucerne patch and potato patch ; here also grow the roots, the sweet corn for the house, and all the green fodder used for summer, as well as some to dry.

The men kept are : the foreman, who is a thorough proficient at his business, as the healthy condition of the herd, the honors won in show rings, and the excellent quality of the butter can testify.

He assists with the milking, feeds the calves, strains and skims all the milk, makes and ships all the butter (thousands of pounds yearly), makes out the invoices, and keeps a set of books the duplicates of which are kept by me.

He has, to assist him, an intelligent and industrious young man, who is a capital milker.

On one of the small farms lives the farmer, who is busy on farm all summer, and has extra help in haying and harvest.

In winter the farmer helps to milk, night and morning. In the forenoon he helps grooming the cattle, and cleans out the barns; and in the afternoon draws out manure, or goes for sawdust, of which we use a good deal for bedding.

The number of cattle kept averages 54, and a pair of strong farm horses and a few pigs complete the list of farm animals.

A great deal of cream is sold to confectioners who send to the Dairy for it, paying 35 cents a quart in summer and 40 cents in winter. People who take but a single quart pay 50 cents for it, and sometimes we cannot meet the demand.

# CHAPTER XVI.

## FARM ACCOUNTS.—ODDS AND ENDS.—SOME MISTAKES.

Of course it goes without saying that a strict account is kept of all money paid out, or taken in, on the farm.

Everything is entered in the general Cash Book, and then all items are posted out into the Ledger, each under its appropriate heading.

The two principal headings are, "Farm account" and "Stock account."

In farm account, on one side appears all money spent for rent, wages, feed, extra help, seed, etc.; on the other side, all cash received for sales of milk, cream, butter, or pork, also a fair market value for whatever amount of these things has been consumed in the family.

In the stock account, on one side, is entered every animal bought, under its own name and number; the name and address of the person from whom it was bought, date, and price paid. On the other side is entered, in a similar manner, every animal sold, name and address of purchaser, and price paid.

A farm book is also kept, giving date when each calf is dropped, also name of sire and of dam.

A Dairy book is also kept, in which are the daily entries of milk, cream, or butter sold, to whom, and what price received.

These are all that are really necessary to show how one stands at the end of each year, and they are all I have time for.

One thing is very laborious, and that is the large correspondence about cattle. I tried keeping a catalogue of my herd, but 1000 went off in a short time, and, besides, so many changes take place in a herd, as animals grow up, are sold, or replaced by others, that it is difficult to keep a catalogue in shape.

I have, however, extended pedigrees, printed, of my chief animals, so it is always easy to send pedigree of sire and dam of a calf.

And if you keep thoroughbred stock, you must make up your mind to answer all business letters promptly, fully, and cheerfully.

It is a courtesy which your customers have a right to expect, and which *you* would expect were you buying valuable cattle from them.

And, in describing an animal, be sure to represent it exactly as it is. I know of few greater pleasures than to get a letter saying a customer is perfectly and entirely satisfied, and finds the animal he has received to be even better than represented.

If you have a worthless animal, send it to the butcher, without hesitation, it will be a saving in the end.

Keep only the very best. With all your care and skill in breeding you will still find a difference in your herd.

If you are fortunate enough to have no bad ones, you will still have good, better, and best; therefore, in selling, state exactly what each animal is, and if purchase is made by a party who does not see the cattle, but who leaves it to you to choose for him, make it a point of honor to give him even better value for his money than if he were present.

In looking back over the past few years, I am sometimes ashamed and sometimes amused at the mistakes I have made, especially in the beginning of my dairy experience.

Working without a thermometer was one, and a very bad one it was. Overworking my butter was another. Still another was buying stock without seeing it, from an unreliable party. This only happened to me twice, but it will never happen again. One animal *had been* good, but her udder was completely destroyed by garget, and I sold her for less than a fourth of what I paid for her.

Another had a long pedigree and a still longer price, but I sold her to a butcher for $22.50, and was well rid of her!

So I bought my experience dearly.

In fact, there is hardly anything against which I have cautioned you that has not been a rock ahead of me at one time or another.

Sometimes I saw the danger in time, and steered clear of it.

But sometimes I didn't, and then the result was disastrous.

In conclusion, *I wish* I could have written this little book without talking so much about myself, but it is in answer to hundreds of questions as to "how I do it," and so I can't help the egotism.

Nor is that the only fault of my work—of this, I am painfully conscious, but I can only ask my readers to lose sight of me (if I have left them any chance to do so), to look at the actual facts in my book and not at the imperfect manner of telling them, and to work on steadily to that high standard towards which I am still struggling myself.

THE END.

# THE AUTOMATIC KNIFE CO. OF ONTARIO

## (LIMITED.)

## GANANOQUE.

**D**O not forget to ask your Hardware Dealer for an **AUTOMATIC KNIFE**; if he should be out of them, have him send for some, or send for one yourself.

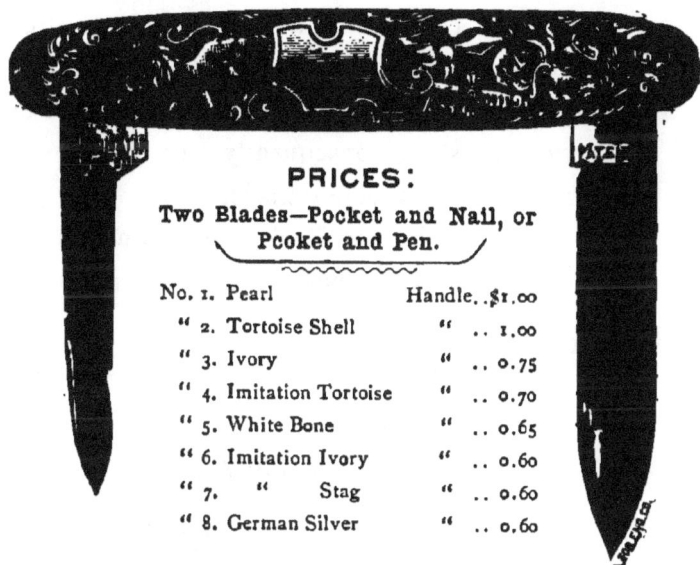

## PRICES:

**Two Blades—Pocket and Nail, or Pcoket and Pen.**

| No. 1. Pearl | Handle | $1.00 |
|---|---|---|
| " 2. Tortoise Shell | " | 1.00 |
| " 3. Ivory | " | 0.75 |
| " 4. Imitation Tortoise | " | 0.70 |
| " 5. White Bone | " | 0.65 |
| " 6. Imitation Ivory | " | 0.60 |
| " 7. " Stag | " | 0.60 |
| " 8. German Silver | " | 0.60 |

**W**E will forward one or more to any address on receipt of price. If you wish to have it registered, send 5 cents extra.

**AGENTS WANTED IN CANADA.**

# BEAVER BRAND

# ASHES.

EXPORTED BY RAIL ON SHORT NOTICE BY

# CHARLES STEVENS,

## NAPANEE, Ontario, Canada.

I WOULD respectfully call your attention to my "Beaver Brand" Canada, Unleached, Hardwood Ashes, which contain from 70 to 80 per cent. of ACTUAL PLANT FOOD in the form of Potash, Phos. Acid, Vegetable Lime, Iron, Soda, Silica, etc. They are thoroughly sifted, which removes charcoal and other debris with which ordinary ashes are filled, and being gathered under my personal supervision and stored in good buildings awaiting shipment, I can positively guarantee them free from "*adulteration*" and *pure unleached*, which makes them the cheapest and best general fertilizer in use, and for grass lands they are unequalled. As a lawn dressing they are particularly desirable, being odorless and easily applied, and their effects are noticeable for years.

I can furnish car lots in bulk or barrels; and small lots in barrels only. Price list and descriptive pamphlet free on application.

Address

## CHARLES STEVENS,

### DRAWER 700

## NAPANEE, Ontario, Canada,

# COOK * BOOK!!

∴ CONTAINING ∴

## 1000 TRIED RECEIPTS,

CONTRIBUTED BY THE

## Ladies of Grace Church,

GRAND RAPIDS, MICHIGAN,

IN AID OF THE

## RECTORY FUND.

PRICE, 75 CENTS.

FOR SALE BY

### MRS. CHILION JONES, Brockville, Ontario, Can.

ALSO BY

### MRS. F. C. STRATTON: Grand Rapids, Mich., U.S.

# S. J. WHITE & CO.,

## BELLEVILLE, ONTARIO,

MANUFACTURERS OF

# PARAFFINED CYLINDER BUTTER BOXES,

## Oyster and Syrup Pails, Berry
## Boxes and Baskets, Axle Grease Boxes,

. . : AND ALL KINDS OF . . .

# THIN WOOD BOXES AND PAILS,

## BOTTLE CAPSULES, Etc.

---

These elegant and substantial butter packages range in capacity from "One" to "Twenty Pounds," they are manufactured from pure tasteless wood selected expressly for the purpose, and are coated inside with a pure, colorless, tasteless and odorless paraffine wax, which entirely prevents the butter from sticking to or in any way coming in contact with the wood; they preserve the butter perfectly air tight and entirely free from woody flavor, and secure from external influences of every kind. Each package may be opened, examined and closed again air tight, and may be kept in any convenient cool dry place without risk of the butter getting any taint from food, impure air or odors of any kind.

*See Page 37 for Reference.*

www.ingramcontent.com/pod-product-compliance
Lightning Source LLC
Chambersburg PA
CBHW021525270326
41930CB00008B/1102